# PORTUGUESE STUDIES

VOLUME 30 NUMBER 2
2014

João Cabral de Melo Neto
(1920 1999)

*Founding Editor*
HELDER MACEDO

*Guest Editor*
SARA BRANDELLERO

*Editors*
FRANCISCO BETHENCOURT
PAULO DE MEDEIROS
PAUL MELO E CASTRO
HILARY OWEN
JULIET PERKINS
LÚCIA SÁ
DAVID TREECE
ABDOOLKARIM VAKIL

*Editorial Assistant*
RICHARD CORRELL

*Production Editor*
GRAHAM NELSON

MODERN HUMANITIES RESEARCH ASSOCIATION

# PORTUGUESE STUDIES

*A peer-reviewed biannual multi-disciplinary journal devoted to research on the cultures, literatures, history and societies of the Lusophone world*

International Advisory Board

DAVID BROOKSHAW — MARIA MANUEL LISBOA
JOÃO DE PINA CABRAL — KENNETH MAXWELL
IVO JOSÉ DE CASTRO — LAURA DE MELLO E SOUZA
THOMAS F. EARLE — MARIA IRENE RAMALHO
JOHN GLEDSON — SILVIANO SANTIAGO
ANNA KLOBUCKA

*Portuguese Studies* and other journals published by the MHRA may be ordered from JSTOR (http://about.jstor.org/csp). The journal is also available to individual members of the Modern Humanities Research Association in return for a composite membership subscription payable in advance. Further information about the activities of the MHRA and individual membership can be obtained from the Honorary Secretary, Dr Barbara Burns, School of Modern Languages and Cultures, University of Glasgow, Bute Gardens, Glasgow G12 8RS, or from the website at www.mhra.org.uk.

Disclaimer: Statements of fact and opinion in the content of *Portuguese Studies* are those of the respective authors and contributors and not of the journal editors or of the Modern Humanities Research Association (MHRA). MHRA makes no representation, express or implied, in respect of the accuracy of the material in this journal and cannot accept any legal responsibility or liability for any errors or omissions that may be made.

Parts of this work may be reproduced as permitted under legal provisions for fair dealing (or fair use) for the purposes of research, private study, criticism, or review, or when a relevant collective licensing agreement is in place. All other reproduction requires the written permission of the copyright holder who may be contacted at rights@mhra.org.uk.

ISSN 0267–5315 (print) ISSN 2222-4270 (online)
ISBN 978-1-78188-123-1

© 2014 THE MODERN HUMANITIES RESEARCH ASSOCIATION

# Portuguese Studies Vol. 30 No. 2

# João Cabral de Melo Neto (1920–1999)

## CONTENTS

| | |
|---|---|
| Preface | 123 |
| Introduction<br>SARA BRANDELLERO | 124 |
| Eros, Love, and the (Anti-) Lyric in João Cabral<br>MARTA PEIXOTO | 128 |
| Journeys and Landscapes in João Cabral de Melo Neto<br>SARA BRANDELLERO | 143 |
| Epistolary Connections: João Cabral and Murilo Mendes<br>CARLOS MENDES DE SOUSA | 159 |
| *Auto do frade* by João Cabral de Melo Neto: A Trope of the Passion<br>VINICIUS MARIANO DE CARVALHO | 174 |
| The Extreme and Geometry: Notes on João Cabral de Melo Neto's Collection on Bullfighting and his Poetic Imagery<br>FLORA SÜSSEKIND | 189 |

\* \* \* \* \*

| | |
|---|---|
| Tactics of Attraction: Saints, Pilgrims and Warriors in the Portuguese Reconquista<br>JONATHAN WILSON | 204 |
| An Inter-disciplinary Africanist: Patrick Chabal<br>DAVID BROOKSHAW | 222 |
| A Literature Waiting in the Wings for History: A Tribute to Patrick Chabal<br>MARGARIDA CALAFATE RIBEIRO | 226 |
| Abstracts | 231 |

# NOTES FOR CONTRIBUTORS

Articles to be considered for publication may be on any subject within the field but must not exceed 7,500 words, and should be submitted in a form ready for publication in English, sent as an email attachment to the Editorial Assistant at richard.correll@kcl.ac.uk.

Contributions whose standard of English is inadequate will be returned. Any quotations in Portuguese must be accompanied by an English translation. Submissions in Portuguese may be considered, but publication will be conditional on provision of a satisfactory translation at the author's expense. The Editorial Assistant may undertake translations on request for a reasonable charge.

Text and references should conform precisely to the conventions of the *MHRA Style Guide*, 3rd edn, 2013 (978-1-78188-009-8), £6.50, US $13, €8, obtainable in print or online version from www.style.mhra.org.uk. All articles are subject to independent, anonymous peer review by experts in the field; authors receive written feedback on the editors' decision and guidance on any revisions required. *Portuguese Studies* regrets it must charge contributors for the cost of corrections in proof deemed excessive.

It is a condition of publication in this journal that authors of articles and reviews assign copyright, including electronic copyright, to the MHRA. Inter alia, this allows the General Editor to deal efficiently and consistently with requests from third parties for permission to reproduce material. The journal has been published simultaneously in printed and electronic form since January 2001. Permission, without fee, for authors to use their own material in other publications, after a reasonable period of time has elapsed, is not normally withheld. Authors may re-publish contributions on a personal website or in an academic institution's digital repository without seeking further permission from the Association, but no earlier than 24 months after publication by the MHRA.

Books for review should be sent to: Reviews Editor, *Portuguese Studies*, Dr Paul Melo e Castro, School of Modern Languages and Cultures, University of Leeds, Leeds LS2 9JT.

# Preface

We are pleased to present the current number, 'João Cabral de Melo Neto (1920–1999)', as this year's thematic issue, and are grateful to our Guest Editor Sara Brandellero for preparing and presenting this body of work, which arose from a symposium marking the tenth anniversary of the Brazilian poet's death.

The issue also includes Jonathan Wilson's reassessment of the Portuguese strategy, following the 1147 conquest of Lisbon, of attracting northern European crusaders to fight on their frontier with Islam, and the role of saintly cults in this policy; and two tributes to the renowned scholar of Lusophone African Politics, History and Literature Patrick Chabal, whose sad death earlier this year we announced in the last issue of *Portuguese Studies*. These tributes, by David Brookshaw and Margarida Calafate Ribeiro, were among contributions to a one-day event, 'In Memoriam: Patrick Chabal, His Life and Works', held at King's College London on 6 June 2014.

We are delighted to welcome three new members to the Editorial Board of *Portuguese Studies*: Hilary Owen, Professor of Portuguese and Luso-African Studies at the University of Manchester, Paulo de Medeiros, Professor of Modern and World Literatures at the University of Warwick, and Dr Paul Melo e Castro, Lecturer in Portuguese at the University of Leeds. Paul is taking on a special role as Editor of our newly reinstated Reviews Section, which will make its first appearance in 2015.

On a more sombre note, we record with great sadness the loss of Professor R. C. Willis, known as Clive Willis to his colleagues and friends, who passed away on 18 April 2014. Emeritus Professor at the University of Manchester, Clive was a specialist in Camões, the Portuguese sixteenth-century epic and lyric poet, as well as being a fine scholar of the Peninsular Wars of the eighteenth and nineteenth centuries and, as a linguist and grammarian, the author of the classic text-book *An Essential Course in Modern Portuguese* (London, 1965). Most recently, he became an outstanding academic translator and a major collaborator on the Fernão Lopes Translation Project, the first full English translation of the fifteenth-century Portuguese chronicler's work. Clive will be much missed as a major contributor to the development of Portuguese Studies in the UK.

THE EDITORS

# Introduction

This special issue of *Portuguese Studies* is devoted to João Cabral de Melo Neto (1920–1999), one of Brazil's most innovative and influential literary and cultural figures. Cabral ranks among the country's giants of twentieth-century literature, alongside such trailblazing authors as João Guimarães Rosa (1908–1967) and Clarice Lispector (1920–1977). His standing as one of the most original voices within the Brazilian Modernist poetry movement, alongside fellow Modernists such as Manuel Bandeira (1886–1968) and Carlos Drummond de Andrade (1902–1987), is undisputed. Indeed, in his lifetime, the wide recognition of his standing included his election as a member of the prestigious Academia Brasileira de Letras [Brazilian Academy of Letters], in 1969.[1] Thus, Cabral features prominently in syllabi of Brazilian literature courses at home and abroad, and the bibliography on his work is extensive. That said, recent studies in English are relatively limited, and this selection of essays aims to help to plug this gap.

The project stems from a symposium organized jointly by Professor David Treece and Dr Sara Brandellero entitled 'João Cabral de Melo Neto and His Transnational Legacy: Dialogues and Confluences', held at Canning House in London in 2009, to mark the tenth anniversary of João Cabral's death. Generously supported by King's College London and the Brazilian Ministry of Foreign Affairs via its Embassy in London, the event provided a forum to reflect on Cabral's work and to seek out fresh perspectives on his writing. Most of the articles included here, all authored by experts in Brazilian literature, were first presented at that symposium or emerged from discussions around it.

Born into a wealthy landowning family from the North-Eastern state of Pernambuco, Cabral was raised on the family's rural estates on the outskirts of the Pernambucan capital city of Recife and later lived in Recife itself, where he went to further his studies. The experience of life in both the rural outback and the city exposed Cabral to the historic social inequalities and injustice of the deeply fractured North-Eastern society, a reality which was to become a recurring *topos* in his poetry. His earliest writings, among them his first

---

[1] Alongside this recognition, it is pertinent to recall some of the many translations of his work. Translations into English include *An Anthology of Twentieth-Century Brazilian Poetry*, ed. by Elizabeth Bishop and Emanuel Brasil (Middletown, CT: Wesleyan University Press, 1972); *Two Parliaments and Poems*, trans. by Richard Spock, in *Brazilian Painting and Poetry* (Rio de Janeiro: Spala, 1979); *A Knife all Blade: or Usefulness of Fixed Ideas*, trans. by Kerry Shawn Keys (Camp Hill, PA: Pine Press, 1980); *Selected Poetry, 1937–1990*, ed. by Djelal Kadir and trans. by Elizabeth Bishop and others (Hanover, NH: Wesleyan Press, 1994); *Death and Life of Severino*, trans. by John Milton (São Paulo: Plêiade, 2003); *Education by Stone. Selected Poems*, trans. by Richard Zenith (New York: Archipelago Books, 2005).

published collection, *Pedra do sono* (1942), which was markedly dreamlike in tone and imagery, gave little indication of the deeply committed social writing which he would produce from the 1950s onwards and with which he would become widely associated.

Cabral entered the diplomatic service in 1946, and his first posting abroad, as Brazilian Vice-Consul in Barcelona in 1947, would have a profound impact on his writing. Away from his native North-East, it was in Spain that Cabral found the clarity and distance to reflect critically on the reality he had left behind, and the works produced during and soon after his first period abroad are amongst his most well-known. *O cão sem plumas* (1950), followed by *O rio* (1954), both have as their central themes the hunger, poverty, the harsh climate, and the lack of land reform and social exclusion that constituted daily struggles for a large majority of the population in the region when these works were published, as they continue to be to this day. These works would be followed by his first *auto* (or one-act play), *Morte e vida severina* (1956), which famously projected Cabral onto the international stage with its uncompromising portrayal of the plight of the play's eponymous protagonist, the migrant and landless rural worker, Severino. The people and landscapes of North-East Brazil would feature prominently in Cabral's poetry, as did the others he came into contact with during his long career in the diplomatic service: England, France, Senegal, Ecuador, to name a few. Among these, as is well known, was Spain, and particularly Andalusia, central theme of his last published collection, *Sevilha andando* (1990).

Cabral's 1966 collection, *A educação pela pedra*, was awarded the prestigious Jabuti Prize, one of many accolades he received during his writing career, including the Camões Prize for Literature (1990), the Neustadt International Prize for Literature (1992) and the Queen Sofia Prize for Ibero-American Literature (1994). It would seal his reputation as a poet of the concrete world, one who found inspiration and reflected on the deepest human concerns through the most prosaic motifs, conventionally perceived as unpoetic objects and situations. One of the collection's most renowned poems, 'Num monumento à aspirina', epitomizes the poet's ability to tease out unexpected meanings from the most ordinary and mundane. The poet himself was keen to foster such perspectives on his writing, emphasizing his rejection of sentimentality, his pursuit of the 'unmelodic', and his position at the margins of Brazil's poetic tradition. In his acceptance speech for the Neustadt prize, the poet declared his wish to avoid any association with the 'clube dos líricos' [the lyrics' club], which he stated constituted the majority.[2] These features of his work have yielded a substantial number of important studies, including a book-length survey by one of the contributors to this issue, **Marta Peixoto**. Her book entitled *Poesia com coisas* focused on the significance of the concrete object in Cabral's work

[2] 'Agradecimento pelo prêmio Neustadt', in *Obra completa* (Rio de Janeiro: Nova Aguilar, 1994), pp. 799–800 (p. 800).

and uncovered the tensions and the often unstable dynamics played out in his poetry.[3] In this special issue, Peixoto's innovative reading of Cabral, in her essay 'Eros, Love and the (Anti-) Lyric in João Cabral', addresses precisely the poet's repeated protestations of his rejection of lyric poetry. Through a survey of his output from his early writings in *Pedra do sono* (1942) to his last collection, *Sevilha andando* (1990), Peixoto uncovers a long and productive dialogue on Cabral's part with precisely the poetic tradition he purported to banish outright. Peixoto's study of his treatment of *eros* and love thereby provides an important contribution to studies on the author.

The second essay, **Sara Brandellero**'s 'Journeys and Landscapes in João Cabral de Melo Neto', also takes as its starting point established understandings of Cabral's work, in this case his close engagement with the concrete world, to suggest a new perspective which reviews the significance of landscape in his *oeuvre*, with a particular focus on his treatment of the nonhuman. Brandellero's earlier studies of Cabral included the monograph *On a Knife-Edge: The Poetry of João Cabral de Melo Neto*, which revised traditional readings of Cabral as a poet of clarity and precision, and concentrated instead on his use of ambiguity, especially in his political writings, and in particular within gender and postcolonial critical frameworks.[4] That revisionist approach is developed here, in an article which focuses on two of Cabral's works from the 1950s which marked his transition towards a socially engaged writing. *O cão sem plumas* (1950) and *O rio* (1954) both have at their core the theme of the journey and the rural and urban landscapes of the North-East, with the Capibaribe river providing a key thematic thread. The article considers the tangled web of connections between different beings and objects that Cabral's poetry recreates and considers his debunking of dichotomies of human–nonhuman in his search for ethical solutions to the historic ills of his native North-East Brazil.

If landscapes feature prominently in Cabral's work, another salient aspect of his writing is the extensive intertextual dialogues he wove into his poetry with authors at home and abroad. Of these, an important early reference for Cabral was fellow Brazilian Modernist Murilo Mendes (1901–1975), to whom he dedicated his collection *Quaderna* (1960), one of his most celebrated works. **Carlos Mendes de Sousa**, the author of a number of studies on Cabral, and the editor of a recent Portuguese edition of *A educação pela pedra*,[5] here provides a significant contribution to our understanding of the dialogue between the two poets through the study of hitherto unpublished correspondence. In his article 'Epistolary Connections: João Cabral and Murilo Mendes', Sousa's extensive

---

[3] Marta Peixoto, *Poesia com coisas* (São Paulo: Perspectiva, 1983). Other important studies with a similar focus include Antonio C. Secchin, *João Cabral: a poesia do menos* (São Paulo: Duas Cidades, 1985).
[4] Sara Brandellero, *On a Knife-Edge: The Poetry of João Cabral de Melo Neto* (Oxford: Oxford University Press, 2011).
[5] Carlos Mendes de Sousa, 'Pósfacio: Dar a Ver o Poema', in João Cabral de Melo Neto, *A educação pela pedra* (Lisbon: Cotovia, 2006), pp. 119–57.

archival research and detailed analysis of the correspondence unearths valuable insights into the developing friendship between Cabral and Mendes, their mutual fascination with Spain and Spanish culture, and the importance of their exchanges for a renewed appreciation of *Quaderna* itself.

**Vinicius Mariano de Carvalho**'s article '*Auto do frade* by João Cabral de Melo Neto: A Trope of the Passion', considers Cabral's second play, *Auto do frade* (1984), and draws some innovative connections with Cabral's earlier *Morte e vida severina* (1956). While Cabral always claimed to be fiercely anti-religious, both his plays engage closely with religious motifs. In his earlier play, Cabral famously drew on the North-Eastern tradition of the Nativity plays to create a work of strong social critique. In his second play, Cabral sought inspiration in the Biblical narratives of the Passion to construct an equally political work in his rendition of the execution of the Carmelite friar Frei Caneca (1779–1825). Frei Caneca, a journalist and scholar, became one of Brazil's most eminent revolutionaries against the rule of Emperor Dom Pedro I, seen as detrimental to the interests of North-East Brazil. Carvalho studies important mystical references embedded in Cabral's play, particularly the poet's reworking of the seven words of Christ on the cross, revealing Cabral's proficient knowledge of Carmelite mysticism in the literary representation of this important historical figure, and relating this work to Cabral's earlier *auto*.

Similarly to Sousa's study, above, archival research also underpins **Flora Süssekind**'s article which closes the special section of this issue, 'The Extreme and Geometry: Notes on João Cabral de Melo Neto's Collection on Bullfighting and his Poetic Imagery'. Süssekind, the author of some of the principal studies on Cabral, including important archival research into his correspondence with fellow Modernist poets Manuel Bandeira (1886–1968) and Carlos Drummond de Andrade (1902–1987),[6] contributes here with a study which provides fresh insight into Cabral's writing through the examination of a relatively small selection of material on bullfighting, including a series of newspaper cuttings and images, which Cabral began collecting when he first moved to Spain in the 1940s. This little-known private collection, discovered in a second-hand bookshop after Cabral's death, provides, Süssekind argues, important clues as to Cabral's lifelong fascination with bullfighting and its significance for the shaping of Cabral's poetics.

I thank all of the contributors, and also the editors and production team of *Portuguese Studies*, for a fruitful collaboration.

SARA BRANDELLERO
LEIDEN UNIVERSITY

---

[6] Flora Süssekind's many publications on Cabral include *Cabral, Bandeira, Drummond. Alguma correspondência* (Rio de Janeiro: Fundação Casa de Rui Barbosa; Ministério da Cultura, 1996) and her edition of *Correspondência de Cabral com Bandeira e Drummond* (Rio de Janeiro: Nova Fronteira; Fundação Casa de Rui Barbosa, 2001).

# Eros, Love, and the (Anti-) Lyric in João Cabral

Marta Peixoto

New York University

When João Cabral received the Neustadt prize in 1992, his acceptance speech at the Brazilian Academy of Letters made a plea for an enlarged conception of poetry that would go beyond 'confessional lyricism', which, Cabral believed, 'since Romanticism, passes for everything that is considered poetry.'[1] At the end of his career, Cabral still insists as vehemently as ever on staking his position as an anti-confessional, anti-lyrical poet par excellence. In the Neustadt speech, he claims that his own poetry 'has nothing to do with the "lyricism" that has come to be not only the quality of certain poets but synonymous with what is expected of all poets' (p. 603). He deplores the narrowing of poetic genres and materials available to poetry: 'Historical poetry, didactic poetry, epic poetry, narrative poetry, confrontational poetry, all abandoned in favor of a poetry of personal expression of states of mind. Everything has been sacrificed to lyricism and this has been generalized and called poetry' (p. 602).

Cabral's poetic production has certainly escaped such a narrowing; he has written, to much praise and recognition, all the kinds of poetry he lists: historical, didactic, epic, narrative and confrontational. But he has also written, I believe, poetry that falls properly in the domain of the lyric. The lyrical portion of his poetry does not dwell on shifting and passing moods, is not confessional or openly emotional. It is not, in other words, the Romantic lyric. Wordsworth's 'spontaneous overflow of powerful feeling' lies far from the effects it seeks.[2] Yet much of Cabral's poetry implies a forceful, idiosyncratic subjectivity and, yes, an implicit 'powerful feeling' that illuminates and energizes the objects and people it contemplates. In 'Dúvidas apócrifas de Marianne Moore' [Apocryphal Doubts of Marianne Moore], Cabral considers, as he speaks in the voice of the American poet, the unwitting personal revelations that might inhere in seemingly impersonal poetic descriptions: 'Sempre evitei falar de mim, | falar-me. Quis falar de coisas. | Mas na seleção dessas coisas, | não haverá um falar de mim?' [I've always avoided speaking of me, | speaking myself. I wanted to speak of things. | But in the selection of those things, | might there not be a speaking

---

[1] 'Laureate's Acceptance Speech', in *The Rigors of Necessity: João Cabral de Melo Neto, 1992 Neustadt Prize Laureate*, ed. by Djelal Kadir, *World Literature Today*, 66.4 (1992), p. 603.

[2] William Wordsworth, 'Preface to *Lyrical Ballads*', in *Selected Poems and Prefaces*, ed. by Jack Stillinger (Boston, MA: Houghton Mifflin, 1965), p. 460.

of me?].³ In *A escola das facas* [The School of Knives] and later collections, subjectivity becomes more openly personal (though never confessional), embodied, with a quiet consistency, in an autobiographical lyric 'I'. Intensity of feeling and the first-person voice have often been associated with the lyric. Although arguing for a trans-historical conception of the lyric, with certain invariable or at least frequent components, is not without its problems, I agree with Jonathan Culler that it is important to hold on to 'an idea of the lyric as a poetic activity that has persisted since the days of Sappho, despite lyric's different social functions and manifestations'.⁴ Many of the common features of the lyric that Culler points to are readily found in Cabral's poetry, such as 'the hyperbolic forms of address' of lyric poetry, 'from apostrophes to birds and clouds and urns to obsessional addresses to a mistress' (p. 205). Although Cabral's poetry is predominantly descriptive or narrative (modes that can be and in his case usually are interwoven with the lyric), he apostrophizes, we might note, the tides of the Capibaribe river, Seville, Recife and its patron saint, Our Lady of Carmo, as well as poetry itself. Many poems, starting with those of *Quaderna* [Four-Spot], address directly (as a 'tu' or 'você') mistresses or other women; some address writers and artists (Quevedo, Mondrian, Augusto de Campos, Auden, José Américo de Almeida, among others). So we find in Cabral another feature of the lyric that Culler singles out, its 'extravagance', as it performs 'speech acts not recorded in everyday speech and deploying not only meter and rhyme [...] but also its own special tenses such as the lyric present' (p. 205). According to Culler, the lyric also displays a 'memorable language — made memorable by its rhythmical shaping and phonological patterning [...]. The power to embed bits of language in your mind, to invade and occupy it, is a salient feature of lyrics: poems [...] ask to be learned by heart, taken in, introjected or housed as bits of alterity, that can be repeated, considered, treasured, or ironically cited' (p. 205). Cabral's at times harsh 'anti-verso' proffers these invitations as much as other more mellifluous poems by other poets.

It could be objected that the characteristics of the lyric that Culler singles out can also inhere in other art forms, such as song lyrics (not surprisingly, given their same historical roots), certain forms of prose, and other kinds of poetry that Cabral favoured, such as the historical or didactic. But it is perhaps more important to see that the confluence of these salient traits has inhabited the poetry that different historical periods have persistently characterized as lyrical. It is easy to understand that by claiming the badge of anti-lyricism — to the point of wishing that his last poem might be a 'poema perverso, | de anti-lira, feito em anti-verso' ['a perverse, anti-lyric poem | made of anti-verse']⁵

---

³ João Cabral de Melo Neto, *Obra Completa* (Rio de Janeiro: Nova Aguilar, 1994), p. 554. Translation by Djelal Kadir, João Cabral de Melo Neto, *Selected Poetry: 1937–1990*, ed. by Djelal Kadir (Hanover, NH, and London: Wesleyan University Press/University Press of New England, 1994), p. 170.
⁴ Jonathan Culler, 'Why Lyric?', *PMLA* 123.1 (2008), 201–06 (p. 202).
⁵ João Cabral, *Obra completa*, p. 560. Unless otherwise noted, all translations from the Portuguese are mine.

— Cabral wanted to set himself apart from his contemporaries in Brazil, emphasizing his poetic innovations, his commitment to rigour both of form and of observation, and his systematic avoidance of sentimentality. But it is also instructive and illuminating to consider a not insignificant portion of his poetry in the broader context of lyrical practice, where it surely belongs.

I therefore agree with critics who speak of 'a tension-filled lyricism' (João Alexandre Barbosa),[6] or 'a new dimension of lyrical discourse' (Alfredo Bosi),[7] or a 'tamed lyricism' (Lêdo Ivo).[8] Cabral does not of course stand alone in resisting certain versions of the lyric and thereby finding for it new dimensions. Other modern poets, among them Marianne Moore and Francis Ponge, whom Cabral admired, also called the lyric into question, while still at times creating within its framework. Marianne Moore, for instance, famously opens her poem 'Poetry' with the words 'I, too, dislike it'.[9] For these poets, as for Cabral, the negation of lyricism has the value of an ascetic discipline that increases the hunger for the nonself, the objects, creatures and places of the world. Given Cabral's *parti pris* against lyricism, how does he approach poems about sexual encounters, erotic praise and love? Although not all lyric poems deal with love, all love poems draw upon lyric modes, if only tangentially. A closer look at Cabral's love poetry offers an excellent vantage point from which to observe the peculiar lyric processes of a poet who has always been fiercely suspicious of the possibilities for poetry of the kinds of emotions usually symbolized by the heart — derided in one of his later collections as '[o] coração, sentimental e puta' [the heart, sentimental and whorish].[10]

It is symptomatic of Cabral's wariness toward the love lyric that he came to it first by means of poems of ill-fated connection or frustrated desire, *topoi* he later abandoned completely. In Cabral's first book, *Pedra do sono* [Stone of Sleep], only one poem, 'A mulher no hotel' [The Woman in the Hotel], centres distinctly on an erotic encounter and is marked by the surrealist- and cubist-inflected aesthetics of Cabral's early phase. A lyric 'I' speaks in the first person but refers to the erotic partner as 'a mulher que eu não sabia': 'A mulher que

---

[6] João Alexandre Barbosa, *A imitação da forma: uma leitura de João Cabral de Melo Neto* (São Paulo: Duas Cidades, 1975), p. 166.
[7] Alfredo Bosi, *História concisa da literatura brasileira* (São Paulo: Cultrix, 1977), p. 522.
[8] Interview with the poet Lêdo Ivo in Bebeto Abrantes's documentary film *Recife/Sevilha: João Cabral de Melo Neto*. Original Video, 2003. DVD.
[9] Marianne Moore, *The Complete Poems* (New York: The Macmillan Company/Viking, 1969), p. 36. For an excellent discussion of the dialogue Cabral's poetry establishes with Marianne Moore's, see Flora Süssekind, 'Com passo de prosa: voz, figura e movimento na poesia de João Cabral de Melo Neto', in *A voz e a série* (Rio de Janeiro and Belo Horizonte: Sette Letras/Editora UFMG, 1998), pp. 31–54 (pp. 40–45).
[10] João Cabral, *Obra completa*, p. 547. Not much has been written about Cabral's love poetry, to my knowledge. For a commentary that focuses on eroticism ('an analysis of sexual exaltation present in the work of the poet from Pernambuco') with pertinent comments on the lyrical aspects of Cabral's poetry, see Janilto Andrade, *Erotismo em João Cabral* (Rio de Janeiro: Calibán, 2008), pp. 51–98. For a discussion of Cabral's radical de-sentimentalization, see Sebastião Uchoa Leite, 'João Cabral e a tripa' [João Cabral and the Innards], in *Crítica de ouvido* (São Paulo: Cosac & Naify, 2003), pp. 89–92.

eu não sabia | (rosas nas mãos que eu não via, | olhos, braços, boca, seios), deita comigo nas nuvens' [the woman I didn't know | (roses in hands I didn't see, | eyes, arms, mouth, breasts) | lies with me on the clouds].[11] The woman, physically close, seems nevertheless banished from the cognitive sphere and only sporadically accessible to the senses. The odd usage of the verb 'saber' when referring to a person, as well as the instability of lying down on clouds, suggest an oneiric representation, informed by a surrealist aesthetics, of a passing encounter in the hotel of the title. In the poem's enigmatic and elliptic narrative, the woman, an object of suspicion rather than affection, gains disquieting powers. If at first she merges with the landscape, as winds race by her shoulders and weeds grow on her bed, she soon inspires in her partner visions of death, damnation and forcible submission to the practice of dire aggression: 'Terei de esmagar crianças? | Pisar as flores crescendo? | Terei de arrasar as cidades sob o seu corpo bolindo?' [Will I have to crush children? | Step on the growing flowers? | Will I have to raze the cities | moving beneath her body?] (p. 53). The concluding lines direct violence and disgust on the woman herself, her body by now dead and dismembered. 'Hei de achar um cemitério onde um seu pé plantarei. | Vou cuspir nos olhos brancos | dessa mulher que eu não sei' [I shall find a cemetery | where I'll plant one of her feet. | I will spit on the white eyes | of this woman I don't know] (p. 53). It's difficult to imagine what might motivate this violence. Perhaps the very engagement with the lyric theme of an erotic encounter, before Cabral had developed distancing tools to confidently neutralize confession or sentimentality, sets off the anxiety that turns into aggression.[12] In any case, this poem of erotic encounter already presents certain tropes that will reappear in Cabral's love lyrics: the conjunction of a woman's body and elements of a landscape, as well as the overlay of the bodies and souls of women and those of cities. If in 'A mulher no hotel' these tropes are poised between the comical and the grotesque, later Cabral will develop them to positive, even luminous, effect.

The prose poem in three voices *Os três mal-amados* [The Three Unloved Ones] that Cabral published the year after *Pedra do sono*, though not properly a love lyric given its dramatic form, also approaches a lyric *topos* — unrequited love — from a negative and occasionally comical perspective. Taking as a point of departure Drummond's poem 'Quadrilha' [Square Dance] quoted in the epigraph ('João que amava Teresa que amava Raimundo | que amava Maria que amava Joaquim que amava Lili...' [João who loved Teresa who loved Raimundo | who loved Maria who loved Joaquim who loved Lili]), Cabral's poem gives voice to the three victims of unrequited love. Sara Brandellero discusses Cabral's

[11] João Cabral, *Obra completa*, p. 53.
[12] It's interesting to note that 'A mulher no hotel' is one of the twenty-nine poems of the first edition of *Pedra do Sono* that Cabral seemed uncertain about (John Gledson, 'Sleep, Poetry, and João Cabral's "False" Book: A Reevaluation of *Pedra do Sono*', *Bulletin of Hispanic Studies*, 55 (1978), 43–58 (p. 57).) It was left out of the 1968 *Poesias completas*, along with eight others. All of them were restored to the collection in the 1994 *Obra completa*.

initial inability to finish the poem — he had meant to write parts for the women as well — reading this absence of female speakers as the impossibility for Cabral's poetry at that time to give voice to female subjectivity.[13] Two of the women, Teresa and Maria, appear in the poem only as the objects of their would-be lover's obsessions; they have little density and no individuality. The third woman, Lili, Joaquim's beloved, doesn't appear in the poem at all: her wide-ranging corrosive effect is blamed on the destructive power of love itself: 'O amor comeu meu nome, minha identidade, meu retrato. O amor comeu minha certidão de idade, minha genealogia, meu endereço. O amor comeu meus cartões de visita. O amor veio e comeu todos os papéis onde eu escrevera meu nome' [Love ate up my name, my identity, my photograph. Love ate up my birth certificate, my genealogy, my address. Love ate up my visiting cards. Love came and ate up all the papers where I had written my name].[14]

As generations of critics have seen, the real thrust of this poem is metapoetic, three modes of articulating personal experience with the composition of poetry.[15] The monologues of the three male characters proceed not by development but by circling around in the same place, each unaware of the others, caught in the narrow circle of his own obsession, speaking to himself and not to the woman he supposedly loves.

If João and Joaquim can be said to suffer, the latter comically with the hyperbolic devastation of his life, Raimundo, the most curious of the three voices, speaks with tranquil equanimity, having turned to advantage the impossibility of love. Unconcerned with Maria's rejection, he identifies her with a shifting series of unexpected metaphorical places and objects: a beach, the sea, a fountain, a paved field, a tree, a *cachaça* bottle, a book. These identifications might at first seem to follow each other in a chaotic enumeration but soon it becomes clear that their function lies in what they permit the speaker to do and be, and also with what they preclude. In one of her guises, Maria is a blank sheet of paper: 'Maria era também a folha em branco, barreira oposta ao rio impreciso que corre em regiões de alguma parte de nós mesmos. Nessa folha eu construirei um objeto sólido que depois imitarei, o qual depois me definirá. Penso para escolher: um poema, um desenho, um cimento armado — presenças precisas e inalteradas, opostas a minha fuga' [Maria was also a blank sheet of paper, a barrier against the imprecise river that runs in regions somewhere inside us. On that sheet I'll construct a solid object that I'll then imitate and which later will define me. I think so as to choose: a poem, a drawing, a structure of cement — precise and unaltered presences, opposed to my flight] (p. 63). Defined in ways that don't cohere as a human personality, Maria makes creativity possible by

---

[13] Sara Brandellero, '(Dis)covering the Other: Images of Women in João Cabral de Melo Neto', *Bulletin of Hispanic Studies*, 81 (2004), 229–40 (p. 230).
[14] João Cabral, *Obra completa*, p. 59.
[15] See for instance, Benedito Nunes, *João Cabral de Melo Neto* (Petrópolis: Vozes, 1971), p. 46; Barbosa, pp. 35–40, and Marta Peixoto, *Poesia com coisas: uma leitura de João Cabral de Melo Neto* (São Paulo: Perspectiva: 1983), pp. 30–35 and Brandellero, '(Dis)covering the Other', p. 230.

disappearing into objects that can be properly controlled, as in myths where wayward creatures might be punished by being turned into a tree, a river, or a flower. The metaphoric objects do not so much embody Maria as replace her. They open up to Raimundo a world of solid constructions, freeing him from the desiccating, unproductive emotions of loss and deprivation that imprison João and Joaquim. If not convincing as a beloved woman, Maria is quite convincing as a figure that fosters creativity, perhaps an anti-lyric muse, who vanishes taking with her all lyric themes, so that the poet can then articulate the constructed poetry of his choice.

After these early poems of frustrated love, Cabral, for over a decade, turns away completely from lyric themes. The attack on a self-centred, experientially based confessional lyricism takes on intense, vituperative tones in the three series of poems of *Psicologia da composição* [The Psychology of Composition], as in the famous lines 'Poesia: te escrevia: | flor! conhecendo que és fezes, | fezes como qualquer' [Poetry I wrote you *flower!* | knowing that you are feces, | like any other feces],[16] an attack that does not shy away from the complete rejection stated in those other famous lines: 'A flauta | eu a joguei, | aos peixes surdo- | mudos do mar' [the flute, I threw it | to the deaf | and dumb fishes of the sea] (p. 92). Cabral turned productively to other poetic modes, to narrative poems and outward-directed accounts of the landscapes and artists of Pernambuco and Spain, while honing a language based on the articulation and analysis of striking figurative images. Only much later, in *Quaderna* (1960), does Cabral return to the *topos* of love, by then in possession of some of his most characteristic poetic instruments: a playful and somewhat detached tone, visual metaphors and similes, a witty and ever-shifting manipulation of figurative language. 'Mulher vestida de gaiola' [A Woman Dressed as a Cage] speaks of unrequited love — or perhaps more accurately, desire — in a poem that displays Cabral's mature poetic language. With wit and ingenuity, Cabral avoids any hint of sentimentality by etching feelings and experiences — here the negative ones of rejection and exclusion — in sharp visual images. The poet imagines the object of desire surrounded by a cage, whose function is not so much to confine her as to keep her admirer out. This cage, crafted to her exact measurements, covers her like an item of clothing, 'gaiola-blusa ou camisa' [a cage that's a blouse or a shirt].[17] But the poem speaks also of another cage: it imprisons not the love object but the infatuated lover and traps him in a vast external space that excludes him only from the 'gaiola-ilha' [cage-island] (p. 261) confining (or protecting) the woman. That outside space, though in other ways limitless, confines the lover barred from the object of his desire:

---

[16] João Cabral, *Obra completa*, p. 98. Translation by Richard Zenith, *Education by Stone: Selected Poems of João Cabral de Melo Neto* (New York: Archipelago Books, 2005), p. 43.
[17] João Cabral, *Obra completa*, p. 261.

> é como outra gaiola,
> igual que o mar: sem medida
> e aberto em todos os lados
> (menos no que te limita).
>
> Pois nessa gaiola externa,
> onde tudo tem cabida,
> onde cabe Pernambuco,
> e o resto da geografia,
>
> três bilhões de humanidade
> e até canaviais de usina
> sei que se debate um pássaro
> que a acha pequena ainda. (p. 261)

[it's like another cage, | just like the sea, | beyond measure | and open on all sides | except those that limit you. | Well, in this external cage, | where everything has its place | including Pernambuco | and all the rest of geography, | three billion of humanity | and even sugarcane fields, | I know of a bird thrashing about | who thinks it's too small for him.]

The structure of address alters the characteristic 'I'–'you' of so many love lyrics, derailing the more direct, emotional connection it implies. In this poem, the speaker splits himself off from the rejected lover who appears first as the bird that he knows about, constrained and trapped in that vast outside space. Later, in a reconsidered and adjusted metaphor, the rejected admirer becomes a force likened to a flood: 'a sua força expansiva, | (não de pássaro, de enchente, | de enchente do mar de Olinda)' [its expansive force, | (not of a bird but of a flood | of the sea that floods Olinda] (p. 262). The poem, with its crisp visual imagery and cool detachment, deflects onto the bird and the flooding sea the urge, quite forcefully expressed, to penetrate the woman's protected space: 'que deseja assaltar | precisamente a área estrita | da gaiola em que resides' [who wants to assault | precisely the exact area | of the cage in which you live] (p. 262). Amusement rather than desperation marks the dominant tone, yet the insufficiency of the space outside, the flooding impulse, and the fantasy of assault, all convey strong feelings while embodying them in distinct visual forms that curb any possible pathos. The cerebrally constructed and shifting metaphors, of the kind called conceits in that the two terms compared — such as 'woman' and 'cage' — conjoin unexpectedly disparate semantic areas, present the speaker not as another Joaquim, a pathetic being devoured by unrequited love, but as a successful poet in control of his craft who speaks in the present tense, at the very moment of practising it. The poem also enacts a small revenge on the rejecting woman. What's better, after all: to be trapped in a tiny cage coterminous with one's own skin or to range freely in the vast outside space? The pain of unrequited love is figured in such a way that it also hints at its cure.

After 'Mulher vestida de gaiola', perhaps his last poem about unrequited attraction, Cabral's erotic lyrics — poems such as 'História natural' [Natural

History], 'Paisagem pelo telefone' [Landscape over the Telephone], 'A mulher e a casa' [The Woman and the House], 'Rio e/ou poço' [River and/or Well], 'Imitacão da água' [Imitation of Water], 'Jogos frutais' [Fruit Games] and 'Escritos com o corpo' [Written with the Body] — speak in the present tense of joyous connection and fruition, even in casual sexual encounters. They continue to use some of the poetic strategies evident in 'Mulher vestida de gaiola': the conceits that identify women with spatial forms, the adjustments of figurative language as the poem progresses, the variations on the 'I'-'you' structure of address, sometimes altered to 'you'-'he', or even 'she'-'he', and the present-tense focus on the moment of writing. These strategies create a distance that allows the poems to steer clear of confession; they present the poet as the mind that creates and only by inference as the man who feels. These poems centre on desire that finds what it seeks and often dwell explicitly on touching and penetration; the emotional connection, if any, radiates from the physical.

*Quaderna* and later books also offer another kind of love lyric: one in which a woman's body (or soul), artistic language or the impulse toward it, and personal love all become somehow superimposed or enmeshed, and inhabit a spatial image. Unlike what occurs in Raimundo's speech in *Os três mal-amados*, where Maria disappears as a woman to make possible the pursuit of a certain kind of poetry, in these later poems the woman and artistic language are equally vivid and mutually enhancing objects of desire. In 'A palavra seda' [The Word Silk], for instance, the speaker praises both the power of a woman to energize those around her and the power of poetic language to renew a word seemingly worn out by frequent, unimaginative use. The quite intricate logical concatenation of the argument maintains that while nothing in the woman resembles what the word silk conveys in its conventional acceptations, 'a superfície | luxuosa, falsa, acadêmica, | de uma superfície quando | se diz que ela é "como seda"' [the luxurious, | false, academic surface | that surface designated | by the phrase 'like silk'],[18] there is a common ground between the tactile sensation of the object silk and sensorial contact with the woman's skin as well as in the pleasurable tension that the woman's presence brings about: 'no ambiente que retesas quando chegas' [in the ambience | made tense by your presence] (p. 246; p. 113). The vicissitudes of erotic attraction, worn thin by poetic use over the centuries, have also appeared to Cabral, as we have seen, just as 'impossíveis de poema' [impossible in poems] (p. 246; p. 113) as the worn words silk and gold. Focusing on concrete sensory data and — not least — poetic invention through clever metaphoric associations renews the word silk while also renewing and thus rendering permissible in poetry that old *topos* of erotic praise. Although the woman is addressed as a 'you', the subjectivity that constructs the poem (and that the poem constructs) only figures obliquely as an erotic partner, in the impersonal subject of 'tudo | isso que em ti se tateia' [all | that in you can

---

[18] João Cabral, *Obra completa*, p. 246. Translation by Richard Zenith, *Education by Stone*, pp. 113–15. A second set of page numbers in the text refers to this translation; if none is given the translation is mine.

be touched] (p. 246) and as part of the very atmosphere keenly affected by the woman's presence. Recourse to the sense of touch renews the word silk but it is also poetic language, in the cluster of animal metaphors that establish the common ground between silk and the woman, that brings about this renewal. Woman and silk have qualities best conveyed in animal terms, the poem claims, even in their perhaps excitingly dubious aspects ('de cru, de cruel, de crueza' [raw, cruel, crude] p. 247). The poem has recourse at once to the cerebral in its intricate argument, to the physical in its appeal to the senses, and to the powers of metaphor; it constructs a compact eulogy both to the woman and to poetry itself, while avoiding the confessional and keeping sentimentality in check.

Another identification between the desired woman and an artistic language occurs in one section of 'Escritos com o corpo' (Serial), where the woman is compared to a painting by Mondrian. Poetic ingenuity justifies this seemingly unpromising comparison. The poem likens the energy of a woman's physical presence to that of a Mondrian painting: from afar both reveal the 'perfeição da geometria' [perfection of geometry].[19] It is only from close up that the actual painting of Mondrian (not, the poem notes, a reproduction) and the woman's body take on a special vibrancy:

> porém de perto, ao olho perto,
> sem intermediárias retinas,
> de perto, quando o olho é tato,
> ao olho imediato em cima,
>
> se descobre que existe nela
> certa insuspeitada energia
> que aparece nos Mondrians
> se vistos na pintura viva. (p. 295)

[up close, when sight is tactile; | to the quick and naked eye | one can discern in her | an unsuspected energy | revealed by the Mondrian | when seen in the canvas.][20]

But finding a similar energy in a woman and a painting is only the first step; the poem proceeds to establish a hierarchy. The woman's body improves on the power of a Mondrian in that her special, close-up vibrancy can do without colour:

> pode abrir mão da cor acesa
> sem que um Mondrian não vibra,
> e vibrar com a textura em branco
> da pele, ou da tela, sadia. (p. 295)

[can forgo the flame of colors | without which a Mondrian is static, | can vibrate with the texture | of wholesome skin, or canvas.] (p. 117)

---

[19] João Cabral, Obra completa, p. 295.
[20] Translated by Djelal Kadir, Selected Poetry, p. 117. Further references to this poem referred to by page numbers in the text are from this translation.

The naked body and the ingenious metaphors that represent it reveal a poet in possession of his woman as much as he is in possession of his poetic craft.

In an interview with Antonio Carlos Secchin that took place in 1980, Cabral says about the women in *Quaderna*: 'I describe a woman with no biography; what she represented in my life is irrelevant.'[21] At the end of that same decade, however, in *Sevilha andando* [Walking Seville] (1989) Cabral seems to take on a new and rigorous challenge: how to write love poems to and about a woman with a public role in his life, a woman, that is, who *does* have a biography. This book, composed of two parts ('Sevilha andando' and 'Andando Sevilha' [Seville Walking and Walking Seville]), contains in its second part poems about Seville, its people, artists and culture, while almost all the poems in the first part are love lyrics. (Later, in 1994, these two parts, with added poems, become two separate collections.) Cabral dedicates *Sevilha andando* to Marly de Oliveira, whom he had married four years earlier. In the lyric poems from *Sevilha andando*, specific autobiographical details (factual rather than confessional) identify the poet as a man from the North-East of Brazil who has lived in and written before about Seville, and the woman as a small, dark-haired and fair-complexioned woman, born in Espírito Santo, of Portuguese and Italian descent, leaving no doubt, in other words, as to whom those two are supposed to represent. Autobiographical reference plays, then, a crucial role in these poems. By venturing into the dangerous terrain of the personal, Cabral sets out to complicate somewhat his anti-lyrical stance, perhaps with the aim of 'Fazer no extremo, onde o risco começa' [To do it on the edge, where risk begins] (in the words of a poem from *A educação pela pedra* [Education by Stone].[22]

The powerful connection between the two characters and her transformative presence in his life are at issue in most of the poems, sometimes with reference to day-to-day intimacy, such as waking up in bed together. Despite these personal references — and perhaps because of them — Cabral also erects effective barriers against confession. Chief among them is the conceit of the wife as a *sevilhana* [a woman from Seville], played out with variations in most of the poems.

Since *Quaderna*, Seville has made regular appearances in Cabral's poetry. But how does a city in its multifariousness become reduced to a graspable spatial form that can then be compared to a woman? The poem 'Sevilha', from *Quaderna*, speaks of the appropriate fit of the city to the human body, 'A cidade mais bem cortada | que vi, Sevilha; | cidade que veste o homem | sob medida' [The best cut city | I've seen, | A city that clothes man | To his exact measure].[23] But Seville's fit does not accommodate all human bodies; it is made specifically to the measure of its male inhabitant: 'Cortada só para um homem, | não todo

---

[21] Antonio Carlos Secchin, 'Entrevista de João Cabral de Melo Neto', in *João Cabral: a poesia do menos* (Rio de Janeiro: Topbooks, 1999), p. 331.
[22] João Cabral, *Obra completa*, p. 344.
[23] João Cabral, *Obra completa*, p. 252.

o humano, | só para o homem pequeno | que é o sevilhano' [Cut for one man, | not all of humanity, | cut for the small man, | the man of Seville] (p. 252). Because of the city's compact layout and narrow streets, the *sevilhano* inhabits public spaces as if they were private ones. In shifting metaphors, the *sevilhano* uses the city as his house, his bedroom, his clothes, and, at the limit, his sexual partner: 'um corpo que se usa, pelo interior' [a body one uses inside] (p. 253). Seville proffers then a receptive intimacy, likened to the sexual anatomy of the female body. Where does this figuration leave the woman resident of Seville, the *sevilhana*? The self-effacing, sheltering woman this representation of the city would lead us to expect is actually upstaged by another, more vibrant figure. In the opening poem of *Quaderna*, 'Estudos para uma bailadora andaluza' [Studies for an Andalusian Dancer], Cabral's flamenco dancer — fiery, assertive, commanding, defiant — appears in the act of artistic performance. These quite different semantic areas — the receptive and sheltering, on the one hand, and the assertive and challenging, on the other — define Seville and the *sevilhanas* of Cabral's subsequent books, and paradoxically converge in the beloved of his final book, *Sevilha andando*.

While the metonymic or metaphoric conjunction of women and cities, countries or neighbourhoods is familiar in literature and song lyrics — as, for instance, in the *bossa nova* song 'The Girl from Ipanema' — in *Sevilha andando* Cabral diverts this image from its commonplace course by identifying his wife not with her own city but with another one. Despite all evidence to the contrary, the poet asserts that she is 'a sevilhana que não se sabia' [the Sevillian who didn't know it].[24] They have the same manner of walking: 'chama morena e petulante, | dela e da sevilhana andante, | ambas em espiga a cabeça | num desafio a quem seja, | e pisando esbeltas no chão, | ambas, num andar de afirmação' [a dusky and petulant flame, | hers and of the walking Sevillian, | both holding high their heads | in defiance of whomever, | both stepping slender on the ground | both, in an affirmative stride] (p. 631). The poems become means not to convince the love object to love the poet back — an issue, apparently, already settled — but to assent to his imaginative vision: 'Para convencer a sevilhana | surpreendida por essas bandas | quis dar-lhe a ver em assonantes | o que ambas tem de semelhante' [to convince the Sevillian woman | caught by surprise around here | I wanted to show her in assonant rhymes | what both have in common] (p. 631).

An important and by now familiar distancing device in these lines depicts the poet in the act of writing, and not under the sway of intense feelings. He analyses his language rather than any emotion per se. In the poem 'É de mais, o símile' [The simile is too much], he discusses the appropriateness of his figurative language and argues for a step beyond comparison into a complete metaphoric identification of his wife with the city:

---

[24] João Cabral, *Obra completa*, p. 630.

> Assim, não há nenhum sentido
> em usar o 'como' contigo:
> és sevilhana, não és 'como a',
> és Sevilha, não só sua sombra.[25]

[so there's no sense at all | in using 'like' with you: | You are a Sevillian woman, not 'like' one | You are Seville, not just its shadow.]

While the grounds for comparison of woman and city centre on their superlative femininity, contradiction, or at least paradox, marks the definition of what this femininity consists of. It can be manifested, first, in the receptivity and sheltering the city offers: 'a atmosfera de pátio, | o fresco interior de concha, | todo o aconchego e o acolhimento | das praças fêmeas e recônditas.' ('Verão de Sevilha') [the atmosphere of patios, | the cool interior of shells, | all the nestling and receptiveness | of female and hidden plazas. ('Summer in Seville')].[26] The cloth awnings set up in the summer to shield downtown Seville from the fierce sun now accompany the poet in his own home. By virtue of his wife's presence, the bed sheets have become protective awnings: 'eu os reencontrei, esses toldos | nos lençóis que hoje nos enfronham' [I found them again, those awnings, | in the sheets that cover us today] (p. 637).

The other side of Seville's feminine nature offers not protection but a self-confident assertiveness that duplicates the sun's brilliance and subjugating power. In this guise, Seville also takes its spark from the spirit of its women, rather than the other way around. The city and its women challenge and defy:

> Uma mulher que sabe ser-se
> e ser Sevilha, ser sol, desafia
> o ao redor, e faz do ao redor
> astros da sua astronomia. (p. 639)

[A woman who knows how to be herself | and be Seville, be the sun, challenges | what's around her, | and makes what's around her | stars of her astronomy.]

The image of the *sevilhana*'s hair as a black sun conjoins her receptive and assertive sides. The poet lays claim to both these aspects: they are her traits but somehow belong to him and he enjoys them in peaceful conjugal domesticity.

> Ele tem sol mais solar
> que também fere a retina
> mas é doce como a noite
> de onde como que não vinha.
>
> É um sol negro que o acorda
> sem ferir como às avessas
> mas é sol, cada manhã
> e tem dele a cabeleira. (p. 650)

---

[25] João Cabral, *Obra completa*, p. 634.
[26] João Cabral, *Obra completa*, p. 637.

[He has a sun that's more solar | and also strikes his eyes, | but it is sweet like the night | from which unexpectedly it comes. | It's a black sun that wakes him | inversely and without pain | but it's a sun, each morning, | having the sun's luxuriant hair.]

The image of the woman's hair as a black sun alludes to Nerval's 'soleil noir' (though not to its melancholy aspect) and Baudelaire's 'chevelure', as Sara Brandellero has observed;[27] we might also note that this metaphor represents a further step in the trajectory of the sun as an image in Cabral' s poetry. The sun has previously appeared as the harsh sun of the North-East, figuring the manifold troubles of the region, and as the much-prized sun of reason, intelligence and lucidity. Thus Cabral's love lyrics do not break with his practice of intensive exploration of the same chosen images in negative and positive registers, and of always finding in them new meanings.

Besides the contradictory construction of the *sevilhana* and the beloved as offering both shelter and defiance, another paradox lurks in the conjunction of the poet's Brazilian wife and the women from Seville. A consummate femininity justifies the identification between the woman and the city of Seville: 'a cidade criada do chão | que tem o clima que é mister | à mulher para ser mais mulher' [a city raised from the ground | that has the climate that's needed | for a woman to be more of a woman],[28] but this argument has paradoxical implications. If the connection between place and the characteristics it engenders in its people is so necessary and unfailing, how, then, can it be best exemplified in a woman who lives on another continent and has never set foot in the city in question? Here and elsewhere in Cabral, it is precisely where commonplace logic fails that poetic logic triumphs. Given all that has been written about the lucidity and rigour of Cabral's poetry, it's important to remember that his poetic logic leaves much room for irrational leaps and ingenious manoeuvres that in the end always prevail.

Much could be said about gender dynamics in the 'Sevilha andando' poems;[29] I'd like to make just a few more comments. There is certainly something perhaps playfully authoritarian about fitting his wife so neatly into the role of the 'sevilhana' — you *are* what you *are not*, because *I say so*. And is it really the *sevilhana* (and the wife) who make all those around her 'astros de sua astronomia' [stars of her astronomy] (p. 639)? In these poems, Cabral places his wife firmly within his own poetic astronomy by identifying her with Seville, 'fêmea e viva' [female and alive],[30] a city he had been writing about since *Quaderna*. We might also note, on the one hand, the strange de-individuation of his wife — herself an accomplished poet, the author of several books —

---

[27] Sara Brandellero, *On a Knife-Edge: The Poetry of João Cabral de Melo Neto* (Oxford: Oxford University Press, 2011), pp. 176–79.
[28] João Cabral, *Obra completa*, p. 635.
[29] For a broader consideration of gender in *Sevilha andando* and *Andando Sevilha*, see Sara Brandellero, *On a Knife-Edge*, pp. 159–96.
[30] João Cabral, *Obra completa*, p. 456.

distinguished in these poems for what she shares with scores of women half a world away. But, on the other hand, we might also note the intense and self-contained emotion that irradiates from the profound integration of the wife of Cabral's later years into the poetic universe the poet had been creating for decades. As Cabral observes in the poem 'A sevilhana que não se sabia', even before she entered his life she is already all there, 'antevista' [pre-seen] (p. 631) in his earlier poems about Seville. 'Se viver-te será curto' [If living you will be brief], the poet says to his late-in-life love, 'como pequena é Sevilha, | que viver-te seja intenso | carregado qual nova pilha' [as Seville is small | may living you be intense, | charged like a new battery].[31] The intensity of their future together seems to derive not least from the fact that her metaphoric presence reaches far back into Cabral's past as a poet.

The love lyrics in *Sevilha andando* foreground rational construction rather than the free-flowing course of affections. As we have seen, the poetic voice usually speaks at the very moment of engagement with composition and alludes only indirectly to intensity of feeling. Certain motifs — the wife as *sevilhana*, Seville as superlatively feminine, the proud walk of the *sevilhana*, head held high, her hair a black sun — reappear again and again, giving the impression that the poems are generated from a ludic intelligence deploying an *ars combinatoria*, rather than stemming from the urgency of any particular mood or feeling that demands expression. Equally variable, and also deployed permutationally, is the structure of address in the poems: occasionally, the 'I' of the poem addresses the loved woman directly; more often, an impersonal voice speaks to a 'you', or presents the two protagonists as 'he' and 'she', or simply as a 'we.' Or the woman may be entirely subsumed by a metaphoric figure, as she is in the black sun of her hair in the poem quoted above.

To claim that Cabral's love poetry should properly be considered lyrical requires setting aside a definition of the lyric that necessarily foregrounds the expression or representation of the flux of emotions and recalling instead the pre- and post-Romantic lyric that prominently features linguistic play. Cabral's love poems, as the rest of his work, conform completely to his often-stated conviction that 'poesia é engenho' [poetry is inventiveness] ('A Quevedo', *Museu de Tudo*, 394). The mention of Quevedo, whose writings include celebrated love poems, as an example of devotion to ingenious poetic constructions should remind us that these traits are not inimical to the lyric, even to the love lyric. On the contrary, the praise of a beloved or the railings against the disasters of love often serve as occasions for the display of consummate poetic ingenuity and skill. The poetry Cabral has always aimed for, as he states in the concluding paragraph of his Neustadt acceptance speech, requires 'the exploration of the materiality of words and of the possibilities of organization of verbal structures' (p. 603), a characterization remarkably close to another of the traits of the lyric that Jonathan Culler points out: the lyric as a 'patterning of language', as 'a

---

[31] João Cabral, *Obra completa*, p. 642.

linguistic event that foregrounds language in its material dimensions' (p. 205). Cabral's love lyrics amply demonstrate that he deploys this same constructive effort in his lyric poetry. If we set aside Cabral's own narrow definition of the lyric as always and chiefly sentimental and confessional, we can reclaim these poems for the rich tradition of the Western love lyric, to which they make a strikingly original contribution.

I would like to thank Sara Brandellero and David Treece for inviting me to participate in the conference they organized ('João Cabral de Melo Neto and his Transnational Legacy: Dialogues and Confluences', London, 9 October 2009), where I read the first version of this paper.

# Journeys and Landscapes in João Cabral de Melo Neto

Sara Brandellero

*Leiden University*

'a walk is only a step away from a story; and every path *tells*'
Robert Macfarlane[1]

Brazilian poet João Cabral de Melo Neto (1920–99) authored some of the most iconic writings of the country's twentieth-century literature, many of which centred on the landscape and the human suffering of his native North-East Brazil, one of the country's poorest and most socially fractured regions. Cabral's association with the landscapes of his native land and the shift that it entailed towards socially engaged poetry was sealed early on in his career with the publication of three key works from the 1950s: two long poems *O cão sem plumas* (1950) and *O rio* (1954) and the one-act play *Morte e vida severina* (1956). It was with these works and at this time that Cabral emerged as a poet radically committed to the critique of the North-East's history of social neglect.

At the heart of these works is the body of water of the Capibaribe river, one of the most important landmarks in the north-eastern region, which flows from the barren interior to the city of Recife, on the coast. The river's significance in terms of theme and imagery led these works within Cabral's *oeuvre* to be known as the Capibaribe Triptych.[2] Indeed, following *O cão sem plumas* and *O rio*, the river and surrounding landscape are incorporated into Cabral's most famous work, *Morte e vida severina*, which deals with the plight of the North-East's impoverished migrant workers. The play's protagonist, Severino, makes the desperate journey on foot from the arid interior, following the course of the Capibaribe river, in the ultimately futile search for a better life on the coast. It was *Morte e vida severina* which brought Cabral international recognition, particularly after being set to music by acclaimed singer-songwriter Chico Buarque (b. 1944) and the staging by the Teatro da Universidade Católica (TUCA), the São Paulo Catholic University Theatre Company, at the 1966 Theatre Festival of Nancy, where Cabral received the Prize for Best Living Writer. The award sealed what would remain an enduring literary association with the natural world of his native land, the places and their people.

---

[1] Robert Macfarlane, *The Old Ways: A Journey on Foot* (London: Penguin, 2013), p. 18.
[2] First coined by Angel Crespo and Pilar Gómez Bedate, 'Realidad y forma en la poesía de João Cabral de Melo Neto', *Revista de cultura brasileña*, 8 (1964), 5–69 (p. 36).

In this essay, the focus will be on the first two of these three works from the 1950s, considering the role of landscape in the poet's search for ethical solutions. By landscape, I take cultural geographer John Wylie's definition as something which is 'a perceiving-with, that *with which* we see, the creative tension of self and the world'.[3] My contention is that one can identify in Cabral's treatment of landscape a process analogous to that defined by Bruno Latour in his formulations of Actor-Network-Theory (ANT), when he stated that 'no science of the social can even begin if the question of who and what participates in the action is not first of all thoroughly explored, even though it might mean letting elements in which, for lack of a better term, we would call non-humans.'[4] Thus, this article will contend that Cabral's imaginative envisioning of Brazil in pursuit of ethical solutions is anchored in a more-than-human earth-view, an entanglement of beings, 'patterned by both human and nonhuman processes'.[5]

## Matter and the Real

Cabral's uncompromising gaze on the hardship and endemic social contrasts of the North-East mapped a new cartography for the region. Much of his exploration was conveyed through the theme of travel, as he uncovered the signs and traces of human suffering and the trails of displaced peoples etched onto the landscape. Carlos Mendes de Sousa noted how space and landscape, more than just recurring themes in Cabral's work, became its 'forças motoras' [driving forces].[6] Some of the titles of his early works are revealing of such a connection: see for example the collection *Paisagens com figuras* (1956), the poems 'Paisagem pelo telefone' and 'Paisagens com cupim' (*Quaderna*, 1960), as well as the two sections entitled 'Paisagem do Capibaribe', of *O cão sem plumas*, on which I will focus more specifically here. Two landscapes dominated Cabral's *oeuvre*. The first was that of his native state of Pernambuco, in North-East Brazil, of sugarcane plantations, the urban sprawl of Recife, the shantytowns built along the mudflats of the Capibaribe, the drought in the *sertão* [dry hinterland] and the *agreste* [semi-arid interior], the *zona da mata* [fertile land along the coast], the beaches, places where colonial encounters and struggles had been staged. In Cabral's literary journeys, Toritama and other smaller towns dotting the Pernambucan interior were methodically written onto his literary map. The second landscape was that of Andalusia, where Cabral's peripatetic life in the Brazilian diplomatic service took him in the 1950s and which inspired poetry of flamenco dances, of the streets and architecture of

---

[3] John Wylie, *Landscape* (London: Routledge, 2011), p. 217.
[4] Bruno Latour, *Reassembling the Social: An Introduction to Actor-Network-Theory* (Oxford: Oxford University Press, 2005), p. 72.
[5] In Pile et al., *Patterned Ground: Entanglements of Nature and Culture* (London: Reaktion, 2004), quoted in Wylie, p. 205.
[6] Carlos Mendes de Sousa, 'Pósfacio: Dar a Ver o Poema', in João Cabral de Melo Neto, *A educação pela pedra* (Lisbon: Cotovia, 2006), pp. 119–57 (p. 145).

Seville, of bullfighters. Cabral's poem 'Autocrítica', from the collection *A escola das facas* (1980) reflects on his obsessive engagement with these landscapes: 'Só duas coisas conseguiram | (des)feri-lo até a poesia: | o Pernambuco de onde veio | e o aonde foi, a Andaluzia' [Only two things managed to | strike him into poetry: | Pernambuco where he came from | and where he went, Andalusia].[7]

Cabral's poetry is inspired and shaped by the material world. The critic Richard Zenith noted 'the privileged status it accords to things'.[8] Two important literary references in his work are the poets of materiality, Marianne Moore (1887–1972) and Francis Ponge (1899–1988).[9] The critic Marta Peixoto aptly highlighted the visual evocation of its images, inspired by objects from which Cabral drew 'lições de estética e de crítica social e até mesmo preceitos morais' [lessons in aesthetics, social criticism and even moral precepts].[10] Such engagement with the concrete world also underpins John Gledson's insightful reading of the collection *Pedra do sono* (1942), Cabral's first published work and often seen to be at odds with the his subsequent output.[11] Gledson argues that the collection's surrealist tone is only apparent and suggests that *Pedra do sono* is in fact a conscious attempt to reproduce the sensation of sleep: 'For sleep [...] is the perfect case of a state in which the subjective mind becomes its own object, contemplates itself as if it were another being or thing, seeing quite clearly things which it cannot control, though they are part of itself.'[12]

If my main focus is Cabral's evocation of landscape, central too are the human bodies moving through and imprinted in it. Following Merleau-Ponty's phenomenological formulations, anthropologist Christopher Tilley reminds us that 'the body is not an object outside of consciousness but the only way of being present in the world and being conscious of it. In other words consciousness is corporeal.'[13] And he goes on to say that 'the immaterial mind, somehow divorced from the body, is a philosophical mirage or phantom. At the basis of all, even the most abstract, knowledge is the sensuous, sensing and sensed body in which all experience is embodied: subjectivity is physical.'[14]

Cabral seems to recreate just such a connection in another poem of the

---

[7] João Cabral de Melo Neto, *Obra completa* (Rio de Janeiro: Nova Aguilar, 1994), p. 456. All further quotations are taken from this edition unless otherwise stated. Translations are by the author unless otherwise stated and are deliberately literal.
[8] Richard Zenith, 'The State of Things in the Poetry of João Cabral de Melo Neto', *World Literature Today*, 66 (1992), 634–38 (p. 634).
[9] Zenith, p. 635.
[10] Marta Peixoto, *Poesia com coisas* (São Paulo: Perspectiva, 1983), p. 10.
[11] John Gledson, 'Sleep, Poetry and João Cabral's "False" Book"', *Bulletin of Hispanic Studies*, 55.1 (1978), 43–58 (p. 43).
[12] Gledson, p. 45. Still according to Gledson (p. 44), the closing lines of the poem 'Os olhos', for instance, translate the experience of an alienated self, which is at once present and absent: 'Juntos os peitos bateram | e os olhos todos fugiram. | (Os olhos ainda estão muito lúcidos)' [Together the hearts beat | all eyes fled. | (The eyes are still very lucid)] (p. 43).
[13] Christopher Tilley, *The Materiality of Stone: Explorations in Landscape Phenomenology* (Oxford and New York: Berg, 2004), p. 2.
[14] Tilley, p. 4.

collection *A escola das facas*, 'Barra do Sirinhaém', where the body is visualized within the seascapes:

> Se alguém se deixa, se deita,
> numa praia do Nordeste
> ao sempre vento de leste;
> [...]
> sente com o corpo que a terra
> roda redonda em seu eixo,
> [...]
> que há um subir do horizonte,
> que mais alto que a cabeça
> seu corpo também se eleva,
> [...]
> Essas praias permitem
> que o corpo sinta seu tempo,
> o espaço no rodar lento,
> sua vida como vertigem. (p. 433)

[If you let go and you lie down | under the steady eastern wind | of a beach in North-East Brazil, | you feel with your body that | the Earth turns round your axis, | [...] | and you can even feel | that your legs are lifting, | that the horizon is rising, | that higher than your mind | your body also rises, | [...] | These beaches make it possible | for the body to feel its time, | space in its slow turning, | your life as revolution.][15]

Zenith's perceptive analysis of this poem highlights its profound materiality, the potential it uncovers in reaching a greater awareness of our 'own humanity as a thing'.[16] As Zenith argues: 'allowing the body to rise higher than our mind (as occurs in the crucial penultimate stanza), we may be able to touch — at least in certain moments — the physics of time and space, feeling ourselves physically a part of the universal rotation. This is not mystical exhilaration but its contrary. It is the plain realization of an essential tranquillity in our organic substantiality.'[17]

Taking a cue from this reading, it could be argued that Cabral's writing draws us into the complex entanglement of mind and matter, of the agency of human and nonhuman bodies. As such, Jane Bennett's thinking on vital materialism provides conceptual tools helpful in developing a renewed understanding of Cabral's engagement with the real. Bennett argues that:

> the image of dead or thoroughly instrumentalized matter feeds human hubris and our earth-destroying fantasies of conquest and consumption. It does so by preventing us from detecting (seeing, hearing, smelling, tasting, feeling) a fuller range of the nonhuman powers circulating around and within human bodies. These material powers [...] enrich or disable, ennoble or degrade us, in any case call for our attentiveness, or even 'respect'.[18]

---

[15] Translation by Richard Zenith, in Zenith, p. 638.
[16] Ibid.
[17] Ibid.
[18] Jane Bennett, *Vibrant Matter: A Political Ecology of Things* (Durham, NC, and London: Duke

This perspective, Bennett argues, has a fundamentally ethical aim of promoting 'greener forms of human culture and more attentive encounters between people-materialities and thing-materialities',[19] and is arguably productive in thinking through Cabral's socially engaged writing.

Cabral evoked landmarks both imposing and small, and his keen eye on the physical world was equally sensitive to the evocative power of the stones and goats of the *sertão* as to its epic vastness, to the resilient *manducuru* [cactus] of semi-arid *agreste*, as to the *zona da mata* and the rolling sugarcane plantations along the coastline. In one of Cabral's early poems, from the 1956 collection *Paisagens com figuras*, for example, the human suffering of those working the land, inconspicuous to the naked eye drawn to the lusciously green plains, would be re-inscribed into the landscape through his compelling evocation of a single sugarcane plant, embodiment of the anonymous and socially invisible plantation worker:

> Não se vê no canavial
> nenhuma planta com nome,
> nenhuma planta maria,
> planta com nome de homem.
>
> É anônimo o canavial,
> sem feições, como a campina;
> é como um mar sem navios,
> papel em branco de escrita. (p. 150)

[One does not see in the sugarcane plantation | any plant that has a name, | no plant called maria, | no plant with human name. || The plantation is anonymous, | featureless, like the plains; | like a sea clear of vessels, | a blank sheet of paper.]

The association between landscape and writing established at the close of the second stanza is in fact a motif in Cabral's poetry, in which the mapping out of the land frequently triggers a reflection on the practice of composition. If landscape and writing were always connected, this was not just in relation to his native North-East but also other lands Cabral encountered throughout his roving life as a career diplomat. One might recall, for instance, the pun in the title of the early poem 'Paisagem tipográfica' (of the collection *Paisagem com figuras*) in which he conjured up tantalizing similarities between the lay of the land of Catalonia's encroaching industrial districts and the practice of typesetting: 'bairros industriais | com poucas margens em branco' [industrial neighbourhoods | with narrow white margins] (p. 160).

In order to explore Cabral's connections between landscape and writing, I will return to his earliest engagements with the land through the works in the Capibaribe Triptych, which will be the focus of the following sections.

---

University Press, 2010), p. 14 [ebook].
[19] Bennett, p. 15.

## O cão sem plumas

Cabral joined Brazil's diplomatic service in 1945 and his first posting was to Spain. The move abroad enabled him to reconsider objectively the landscapes and human reality that he had left behind in his native North-East, which would become recurring *topoi* in his work. Some of his best-known works centred on North-East Brazil were written during or shortly after his early years in Spain. *O cão sem plumas* (1950) and *O rio* (1954) stem from his poetic awakening to the poverty and social injustice suffered by many North-Easterners. The former poem is centred on the river as it flows through the city of Recife, capital of Cabral's native state of Pernambuco, introducing a landscape of extreme poverty for those living in the shantytowns erected along its banks and drawing subsistence from its waters. Divided into four sections — Paisagem do Capibaribe I & II, Fábula do Capibaribe and Discurso do Capibaribe — the poem follows the final part of the river's journey before it flows into the sea.

The turning point which led to the writing of *O cão sem plumas* occurred during his posting in Barcelona, when Cabral was shocked by some statistics he came across in the journal *O observador econômico e financeiro* revealing life expectancy in Recife to be twenty-eight years, lower than the twenty-nine years recorded in India.[20]

Such a social crisis was captured in the opening lines of *O cão sem plumas*, in the section entitled 'Paisagem do Capibaribe' [Landscape of the Capibaribe], through a series of images conjured up through startling approximations. One can detect in the unusual connections established at the outset of the poem the gaze of a poet from which the layers of habit have been peeled back to reveal a reality looked at afresh, in a process of defamiliarization.[21] Thus, the seemingly disparate images of a dog, a street, a piece of fruit and a striking sword conjure up Cabral's almost nightmarish evocation of his native city of Recife as a deeply fractured and violent urban space:

> A cidade é passada pelo rio
> como uma rua
> é passada por um cachorro;
> uma fruta
> por uma espada.
> [...]
>
> Aquele rio
> era como um cão sem plumas. (p. 105)

---

[20] 'Entrevista de João Cabral de Melo Neto', in Antonio C. Secchin, *João Cabral: a poesia do menos* (São Paulo: Duas Cidades, 1985), pp. 299–307 (p. 302).

[21] I draw on the well-known concept of 'defamiliarization' as a key element of art developed by Viktor Shklovsky and the Russian Formalist movement. See Viktor Shklovsky's key essay 'Art as Technique', in *Russian Formalist Criticism: Four Essays*, ed. and trans. by Lee T. Lemon and Marion J. Reiss (Lincoln: University of Nebraska Press, 1965), pp. 3–24.

[The city is crossed by the river | like a road | is crossed by a dog; | a fruit cut by a sword. || That river | was like a dog without feathers.]

The opening stanza introduces a series of relational dynamics to translate the effective nature of those existing on the fringes of life and society. According to Peixoto, the images are defined by the violence and distortions reflecting the social failings which precipitate the dehumanizing impact of poverty.[22] The poet's attraction to the relational dynamics is clear in these opening lines, which establish a series of comparisons in which seemingly disparate beings and objects dramatically collide. Cabral chose to convey these dynamics through the use of verbs in the passive form which intensifies the experience of violence, in turn increased by the elliptical nature of the closing line of the first stanza, in which the mutilated existence of the 'cão sem plumas' is thereby syntactically conveyed. Thereafter, from the relations described in the opening stanza, the poem gradually develops the image of the dog and relates it to that of the river:

> O rio ora lembrava
> a língua mansa de um cão,
> ora o ventre triste de um cão,
> ora o outro rio
> de aquoso pano sujo
> dos olhos de um cão. (p. 105)

[The river now reminded me | of the tame tongue of a dog, | now of the sad belly of a dog, | now of the other river | that of the soaking dirty cloth | of the eyes of a dog.]

The lines operate a shift back in time, revealing the connection between the present impasse (conveyed through the use of the present tense in the opening stanza) and the past retrieved through memory, in the second. The startling connections established in this imagery set the tone in a poem which will progressively dissipate the boundaries between the human and nonhuman in which water, mud, persons, dogs, crabs, sticks become complicated in a mesh of relations of a common landscape of deprivation and neglect:

> Entre a paisagem
> (fluía)
> de homens plantados na lama;
> de casas de lama
> plantadas em ilhas
> coaguladas na lama;
> paisagem de anfíbios
> de lama e lama. (p. 108)

[In the landscape | (it flowed) | of men planted in the mud; | of houses of mud | planted on islands | coagulated in mud; | amphibious landscape | of mud and mud.]

---

[22] Peixoto, p. 92.

The vision of the landscape hinges of the connection between the human and natural world, in which the figure of the animal is key. The name of the river itself suggests such interconnectedness, since Capibaribe derives from the Tupi meaning 'place of the capivaras'.[23]

In this landscape, Cabral homes in on the in-between space of the Capibaribe river, which cuts through the city like an open wound, where the poor pick through waste and mud to survive. The shifting from past to present conveys a situation for which there seems to be no prospect of change, as do the use of brackets to enclose the verb 'fluía' [flowed] to reflect the slow-flowing, almost stagnant, waters of the river on course towards its estuary.

The human body is only fleetingly visualized in the first part of the poem through metonymies which allow but a fragmented vision of the human plight, in a reflection of the invisibility of those forced to feed off what the river provides:

> Em silêncio se dá:
> em capas de terra negra
> em botinas ou luvas de terra negra
> para o pé ou a mão
> que mergulha. (p. 106)

[It offers itself silently: | in layers of black earth | in boots or gloves of black earth | for the foot or hand | that plunges.]

Benedito Nunes noted how the river becomes a site in which history's legacy is played out, and in the first 'Paisagem do Capibaribe', Cabral visualizes a body of water — a dog without feathers — as a receptacle of the North-East's colonial past and a history built on privilege and inequality:

> Ele tinha algo, então
> [...]
> algo da estagnação
> das árvores obesas
> pingando os mil açúcares
> das salas de jantar pernambucanas,
> por onde se veio arrastando. (p. 107)

[It had something, then | [...] | something of the stagnation | of the obese trees | dripping their thousand sugars | from the Pernambucan dining rooms, | through which it passed.]

According to Nunes, the river's body of water becomes the 'escoadouro geográfico das águas de lavagem da história regional, com os seus resíduos e detritos, o rio absorve a viscosa economia açucareira, o passado colonial, a nobiliarquia das famílias e os traços culturais herdados' [geographical gully of the waters which wash regional history, with its residue and waste, the river absorbs the viscous sugar economy, the colonial past, the noble family trees

---

[23] Sebastião Galvão, *Diccionario chorographico, historico e estatistico de Pernambuco* (Rio de Janeiro: Imprensa Nacional, 1908), p. 157.

and the inherited cultural traits].[24] This historicized landscape through the image of the dog without feathers leads to the second section of the poem — 'Paisagem do Capibaribe II' — in which the association between river and human experience is explicitly established:

> Como o rio
> aqueles homens
> são como cães sem plumas
> (um cão sem plumas
> é mais
> que um cão assassinado. (p. 108)

[Like the river | those men | are like dogs without feathers | (a dog without feathers | is more | than a murdered dog.]

In their denunciation of the plight of those living on the margins of society, these lines interrogate the very notion of what constitutes the Human in the eyes of the law. Indeed, following Donna Haraway's argument in *When Species Meet*:

> The Animal is forever positioned on the other side of an unbridgeable gap, a gap that reassures the Human of his excellence by the very ontological impoverishment of a lifeworld that cannot be its own end or know its own condition. Following Lévinas on the subjectivity of the hostage, Derrida remembers that in this gap lies the logic of sacrifice, within which there is no responsibility toward the living world other than the human. Within the logic of sacrifice, only human beings can be murdered.[25]

By way of paradox, Cabral's imaginative visualization of the river draws attention to just such a denial of rights and suggest that it is precisely through the perpetuation of the 'unbridgeable gap' referred to by Haraway, in other words through the reinforcement of the dichotomy human–other, that failures in basic life-rights are ultimately legitimized.

Thus, Cabral's rendition of the river and of everything that lives on it challenges dichotomies of this kind, as the metaphor of the mutilated dog is deployed to denounce a common reality. This is reinforced in the third section of the poem — the Fábula do Capibaribe — in which the muddy, almost stagnant, waters of the Capibaribe as it meanders through Recife are visualized as coming under threat from the cleansing force of the incoming tidal sea waters: 'Quer | o mar | destruir no rio | suas flores de terra inchada' (pp. 112–13) [The sea | wants | to destroy the river's | flowers of swollen earth].

River and sea are juxtaposed in this section: on the one hand the Capibaribe,

---

[24] Benedito Nunes, *João Cabral de Melo Neto*, 2nd edn (Petrópolis: Vozes, 1971), p. 67.
[25] Donna Haraway, *When Species Meet* (London and Minneapolis: University of Minnesota Press, 2008), p. 35. In 'The Animal That Therefore I Am (More to Follow)', Derrida asks: 'Do we agree to presume that every murder, every transgression of the commandment "Thou shalt not kill" concerns only man (a question to come) and that in sum there are only crimes "against humanity"?' Jacques Derrida, 'The Animal That Therefore I Am (More to Follow)', trans. by David Mills, *Critical Enquiry*, 28 (2002), 369–418 (p. 416).

site of all that is marginal in society but also a source of life, as the image of the flowers suggests; on the other, the sea against which the river struggles as it resists institutionalized powers, which are visualized though the association of the sea with the image of the flag: 'Como o rio era um cachorro, | o mar podia ser uma bandeira | azul e branca [...] como um poeta puro | polindo esqueletos' (pp. 111–12) [As the river was a dog | the sea could be a flag | blue and white [...] like a pure poet | polishing skeletons]. From an image of disempowerment and destitution, the 'cão sem plumas' is gradually turned on its head. If the sea is progressively associated with images of mortality (as suggested by the skeleton), the river becomes associated with a life force which increasingly emerges as defying control and essentializing classifications. This much is conveyed, still in the 'Fábula do Capibaribe', through the introduction of yet another unexpected metaphorical approximation, this time in the shape of a fruit: 'aqueles mangues | são uma enorme fruta: | [...] invencível e anônima' (p. 113) [those mudflats | are a huge fruit | [...] invincible and anonymous]. What Cabral proposes here seems to have affinities with what Bennett would posit as the 'material agency of natural bodies' (p. 24), operating a shift away from the human–nonhuman binary and the life/matter distinction. In this way, Cabral's worldview in pursuit of social justice reveals points of contact with Bennett's formulations, when she defends the need to 'theorize a vitality intrinsic to materiality as such, and to detach materiality from the figures of passive, mechanistic, or divinely infused substance' (p. 23).

Indeed, the dog-river's journey towards the sea is one of progressive resistance, the denouement of which is captured in the fourth and final part of the poem, significantly entitled 'Discurso do Capibaribe'. As the title itself suggests, Cabral perceives the river and its landscape, inhabited by human and nonhuman beings, as endowed with what Bennett defines as a 'material agency'.[26] Therefore, in this final section of *O cão sem plumas*, Cabral acknowledges agency that is far from a merely human prerogative but ontologically linked to materiality itself, which connects all that exists and is expressed through the perception of its 'density': 'O que vive é espesso | como um cão, um homem, | como aquele rio' [What lives is dense | like a dog, a man, | like that river] (p. 114). The river and everything in it becomes a source of meaning, where trash, dirt and disorder speak of resistance. Drawing on Mary Douglas's anthropological study on the concept of 'disorder', it could be argued that in Cabral's poem it appears as 'potentiality. It symbolizes both danger and power'.[27] In this context, the closing lines encapsulate a provocative vision of the figure of the animal as a boundary-challenging force:

> O que vive choca,
> tem dentes, arestas, é espesso.

---

[26] Bennett, p. 24.
[27] Mary Douglas, *Purity and Danger: An Analysis of the Concepts of Pollution and Taboo* (London: Routledge, 2002), p. 117 [first publ. 1966].

> O que vive é espesso
> como um cão, um homem
> como aquele rio.
>
> Como todo real
> é espesso.
> Aquele rio
> é espesso e real.
>
> Espesso,
> [...]
> (como uma ave
> que vai cada segundo
> conquistando seu voo.) (pp. 114-16)

[What is living clashes, | it has teeth, an edge, it is dense. | That which lives is dense, | like a dog, a man | like that river. | Like everything that is real | is dense. | That river | is dense and real. | Dense, | [...] | (like a bird | that is every second | conquering its flight.)]

It is poignant that Cabral chose the animal as the closing image of a poem in which the need for and possibility of positive action are envisaged. In his seminal work 'The Animal That Therefore I Am (More to Follow)', Derrida argued against essentializing classifications of the animal-human dichotomy and the supposed hierarchical superiority of the human dominant in Western thought. His defence of animals' ability to respond rather than just simply react underpins much of his argument, in which he states that: 'it would not be a matter of "giving speech back" to animals but perhaps of acceding to a thinking, however fabulous and chimerical it might be, that thinks the absence of the name and of the word otherwise, as something other than a privation'.[28]

Seemingly echoing this perspective, and revealing a keen sensitivity for drawing lessons from the nonhuman world, Cabral's first experience with openly committed poetry articulated an imaginative perspective of interconnectedness of things and people, a disruption of categories of subject and object, charting a progress towards empowerment and ultimately allowing for an overcoming of sterile dichotomies, whereby positive outcomes could be envisioned.

## O Rio

Cabral's writing of O cão sem plumas was followed by a long first-person narrative poem, O rio, subtitled 'ou relação da viagem que faz o Capibaribe de sua nascente à cidade do Recife' [or account of the journey that the Capibaribe makes from its source to the city of Recife]. Written in 1953, it is the poem in which the river Capibaribe tells the story of its journey from its source to the sea. Cabral was living in Brazil at the time, temporarily removed from his diplomatic posting to London, between 1952 and 1954, being under

---

[28] Derrida, p. 418.

investigation for suspected communist sympathies. Despite the fraught times in his diplomatic career, Cabral's recognition as a writer was growing, and the poem was well received, winning the Prêmio José de Anchieta marking the four hundred years since the founding of the city of São Paulo.

Written in the traditional ballad form (or *romance*), with lines of five to seven syllables, the poem echoes the tone and structure of the popular poetic tradition of North-East Brazil. Following Manoel Cavalcanti Proença's studies on Brazil's popular poetry, Nunes reminds us how the oral and the written forms of artistic creation were closely linked in this poetic tradition, with poems initially being composed orally and only then transcribed, or dictated to someone else.[29] Such practice is emulated in *O rio*, which, as its subtitle indicates, is meant to be read as the transcription of the river's own recollection of its journey seaward.

From its source at the Lagoa da Estaca to the city of Recife, the Capibaribe records its progress meticulously, referencing place names and landmarks with a local readership or audience in mind, much in the spirit of the tradition of popular poetry of the North-East. Significantly, the proximity with the local landscape is anchored in a worldview of interconnectedness which emerges right from the opening lines of the poem:

> Sempre pensara em ir
> caminho do mar.
> Para os bichos e rios
> nascer já é caminhar.
> Eu não sei o que os rios
> têm de homem do mar;
> sei que se sente o mesmo
> e exigente chamar.
> [...]
> Desde tudo que lembro,
> lembro-me bem de que baixava
> entre terras de sede
> que das margens me vigiavam.
> Rio menino, eu temia
> aquela grande sede de palha,
> [...]
> que águas meninas cobiçava. (p. 119)

[I always thought of taking | the road to the sea. | For animals and rivers | being born immediately means walking. | I do not know what the rivers | share with the sea people; | all I know is that we feel the same | demanding call. | [...] | Of all my memories, | I remember well that I flowed | among lands of thirst | that watched me from the riverbank. | Child-river, I feared | that big thirst of straw | [...] | that desired child waters].

The image of the 'homens do mar' encapsulates that of the 'retirantes', the poor north-eastern migrants who leave the most desolate areas in search of better

---

[29] Manoel Cavalcanti Proença, *Literatura popular em verso I* (Rio de Janeiro: Casa de Rui Barbosa, 1964), quoted in Nunes, p. 80.

prospects in the urban centres such as Recife, and who would be given centre stage in *Morte e vida severina*. It is significant that in so doing, these lines also articulate an understanding of the world as made up of sentient beings, some human, some not, and reflects a geographical imagination for which, as Tim Cresswell states in relation to Actor-Network-Theory, 'divides between human and nonhuman, or sentient and nonsentient, cease to make sense'.[30]

The journey recorded here is not just one through space but also through time, beginning with the river's childhood in the *sertão* to its maturity. Simon Schama argues that landscape cannot be understood outside of memory, when he states that: 'Before it can ever be the repose for the senses, landscape is the work of the mind. Its scenery is built up as much from strata of memory as from layers of rock.'[31] In a similar vein, Cabral's rendition of the Capibaribe's journey across the impoverished North-East is initially conveyed through an act of remembrance and only subsequently as one experienced in the present time. Yet, even when experienced in the present, landscape is where the history of the region is embedded.

Thus, the narrative of the journey begins with the Capibaribe's recollection of life in the interior, where the historic problem of migration to the coastal region is introduced through the river's personal memory. Indeed, the scale of the landscape and of the social deprivation endemic to the region are conveyed by way of a process of personification in which an almost ogre-like figure suggests the perspective of the child-river, for whom the land is threatening and intimidating. A similar process occurs later on, when the river recalls his encounter with the 'terras fêmeas da Mata' [the female lands of the Mata] (p. 119), by which time a process of sexual awakening is implied. In line with this perspective, the pervasiveness of hunger and desolation along the way is condemned through images in which objects come to life in a landscape where humans are mostly invisible: 'vê-se alguma fazenda; | com suas casas desertas: | vêm para a beira da água | como bichos com sede' [you see some fazendas; | with their deserted houses: | they approach the riverbank | like thirsty animals.] (p. 122).

The river is careful to inscribe the region's iniquitous land distribution and not merely the harsh climate of the interior as the root of endemic poverty:

> Passa depois Boi-Seco,
> Feiticeiro, Gameleira, Ilhetas,
> pequenos arruados
> plantados em terra alheia,
> onde vivem as mãos
> que calçando as outras, de ferro,
> vão arrancar da terra
> os alheios frutos do alheio. (p. 125)

---

[30] Tim Cresswell, *Geographic Thought: A Critical Introduction* (Oxford, Chichester and Malden, MA: Wylie, 2013), p. 689 [ebook].
[31] Simon Schama, *Landscape and Memory* (London: Harper Collins, 1995), pp. 6–7.

[Later I pass Boi-Seco, | Feiticeiro, Gameleira, Ilhetas, | small villages | planted in others' property, | where hands live | that by wearing others, made of iron, | go to extract from the land | the fruit of others.]

If the synecdoche is deployed here to zoom in on the exploited labour force working an unforgiving land, once the river reaches the fertile 'zona da mata' later in the journey, a similar device is employed to opposite effect. Indeed, the endemic hunger and thirst projected onto the landscape at the journey's incipit appear to fade only to give way to the greed of the landowning elite in the fertile region of the sugarcane plantations, in which the sugarcane processing plant (*usina*) acquires the physiognomy of a giant, all-devouring mouth in a landscape of similar devastation:

> Mas na usina é que vi
> aquela boca maior
> que existe por detrás
> das coisas que ela plantou
> que come o canavial
> que contra as terras soltou
> que come o canavial
> e tudo o que ele devorou;
> que come o canavial
> e as casas que ele assaltou. (p. 131).

[But it was in the sugarcane plant | that I saw the largest mouth | that exists behind | the other things that it planted | that eats the plantation | that it let loose on the land; | that eats the plantation | and everything it devoured; | that eats the plantation | and the houses it took over.]

The anaphoric repetition echoes the on-going process of appropriation, of 'gobbling up' on the part of the 'usina', by which the historic problem of iniquitous distribution of land and thereby of wealth is visualized: 'tudo planta de cana | para uma só boca de usina' [everywhere sugarcane plants | for just one sugarcane processing plant mouth] (p. 129).

The human presence within the landscape increases once the river reaches Recife, yet the people who inhabit the deprived urban spaces around the Capibaribe remain anonymous 'sem nenhum nome que os distinga' [without a name to distinguish them] (p. 141). And as in *O cão sem plumas*, their precarious existence is visualized through the vulnerable ecosystem of the river's estuary: 'gente | de existência imprecisa, | no seu chão de lama | entre água e terra indecisa' [people | of imprecise existence, | on their ground of mud | in-between water and dry land] (p. 138). Moreover, in the space of the river, the distinctions between animated and inanimate beings appear blurred: 'com meu variado cortejo | de coisas vivas, mortas, | coisas de lixo e de despejo' [with my varied cortege | of things that are alive and dead, | rubbish and discarded things] (p. 137).

Indeed, echoing the earlier composition, Cabral's *O rio* dissolves the boundaries between humans and the natural world as its gaze shifts fluidly from the plight of animals to people and the land. Some of Cabral's visualizations of life in the 'sertão', of the destitution as well as the resilience of those who live there, conjured up early on in the river's account of its journey, exemplify his keen eye for the multifarious nature of things and beings in the mercilessly barren landscape: 'De onde tudo fugia, | onde só pedra é que ficava, | pedras e poucos homens | com raízes de pedra, ou de cabra' [From whence everything fled, | where only stones remained, | stones and a few men | with stone or goat-like roots.] (p. 120).

The permeable boundaries between the human and natural worlds underpinned the construction of some of Cabral's most striking images of North-Eastern Brazil, in his engagement with the region's social failings. With *O rio*, Cabral projected onto the body of water the storytelling consciousness of a popular poet engaged with the plight of the poor and disenfranchised population, while, for instance, concurrently uncovering affinities with the animal world: 'Mesmo que o mar os chame, | os rios, como os bois, são ronceiros' [Even if the sea beckons them, | the rivers, like the oxen, are sluggish] (p. 126). In fact, as the river is attributed with the power of speech, the boundaries between person and object, nature and culture, mind and matter, animality and humanity are transcended in the landscapes recreated in Cabral's poetry; and one might identify a worldview akin to the Amerindian perspectivism studied by Brazilian anthropologist Eduardo Viveiros de Castro and according to which 'the world is inhabited by different sorts of subjects or persons, human and non-human, which apprehend reality from distinct points of view.'[32]

With this in mind, it is possible to trace a coherent progression from *O cão sem plumas* to *O rio* marked by an increasing agency attributed to the nonhuman, notable precisely as Cabral's commitment with social writing gained increased breadth. Having scrutinized the poverty and injustice within the city of Recife in *O cão sem plumas*, Cabral's perspective on the landscape of the North-East in *O rio* took on a broader geographical and historical dimension. Thus, to conclude, it seems pertinent to reflect on the fact that Cabral's most famous work, *Morte e vida severina*, should have emerged only after complicating the Human–Other dichotomy and giving a voice to the nonhuman. Only then would the human subject, Severino, the destitute migrant from the arid interior, take centre stage and tell his story, retracing the crossing of Pernambuco from the *sertão* to the coast earlier narrated by the river and which likewise represented both a spatial and temporal journey.[33] Arguably, the process of identifying the natural world as belonging within a meaningful set of articulations and connections with the human in the landscapes of *O cão sem plumas* and *O rio*

[32] Eduardo Viveiros de Castro, 'Cosmologies: Perspectivism' <http://www.haujournal.org/index.php/masterclass/article/view/106/134> [accessed 15 January 2014].
[33] Mike Gonzalez and David Treece's excellent study of *Morte e vida severina* draws attention to the fact that Severino's journey is also one through time, from the semi-feudal system of the rural interior to the industrialized city of Recife. See 'Severino's Journey', in their *The Gathering of Voices: The Twentieth-Century Poetry of Latin America* (London: Verso, 1992), pp. 253–61 (p. 255).

has significant ethical implications. Among them, as Richard Iveson argues in relation to the human–animal dichotomy, is that 'to dismantle the machinery of power by which 'other' humans are 'animalised'.[34] Moreover, if Cabral's concern was with the human suffering in his native North-East, his gaze was not divorced from a more-than-human view, in full awareness of the impact of the region's endemic problems on the flora and fauna, earth and waterways which inhabit the landscapes he brought to life in his writing. Thus, as a final consideration, it seems productive to reflect on the relevance of Cabral's writing beyond the context of North-Eastern Brazil and in the light of the urgency of rethinking humanity's relationship with the world around us. As such, Idelber Avelar's argument when reflecting on the issue of non-human rights seems relevant: 'The final paradox may very well be that the most powerful critique of anthropocentric reason today comes from [...] narratives structured around the anthropomorphization of animals, spirits, plants, and bodies of water.'[35]

---

[34] In Richard Iveson, 'What is Zoogenesis (3)?: Derrida & Benjamin, introducing animal studies', <http://zoogenesis.wordpress.com/2011/09/25/what-is-zoogenesis-3-introduction-to-animal-studies-derrida-and-benjamin/> [accessed 15 January 2014]. Quoting Kelly Oliver, Iveson cites some important examples of the relevance of this: 'Until we address the denigration of animals in Western thought on the conceptual level, if not also on the material economic level, we will continue to merely scratch the surface of the denigration and exploitation of various groups of people, from Playboy bunnies to prisoners at Abu Ghraib who were treated like dogs as a matter of explicit military policy.' Kelly Oliver, *Animal Lessons: How They Teach Us to Be Human* (New York: Columbia University Press, 2009), p. 38, quoted in Iveson.

[35] Idelber Avelar, 'Amerindian Perspectivism and Non-Human Rights', <http://alternativas.osu.edu/en/issues/autumn-2013/essays/avelar.html> [accessed 10 April 2014].

# Epistolary Connections: João Cabral and Murilo Mendes

CARLOS MENDES DE SOUSA

*Universidade do Minho*

João Cabral de Melo Neto is perhaps the poet I return to most often, and in this article I intend to present some considerations on my reading of his correspondence with fellow Brazilian poet Murilo Mendes, seeking to highlight particular themes and references, mindful of the fact that the letters to which I refer remain as yet unpublished. The dialogue between the two authors provides important insights into their poetic works, and is particularly helpful for understanding the work of Cabral, given that it is discussed most prominently, both in letters addressed to him and those he wrote. Cabral's personality comes across clearly, even when he is referring to others, and this is especially noteworthy when one considers his repeated and vehement defence of the erasure of the self in his poetry.

### Places and Days

The letters enable us, above all, to piece together biographical details related to these authors: from Cabral's itinerant life (the places he visited during his life in diplomatic service and especially his trips to Spain) to Mendes's journeys (his period in Italy, holidays — trips to Portugal and back to Brazil — and Spain, always on the horizon).

Revealing, in this respect, is how Cabral became interested in an autobiographical project Murilo had suggested:

> Quanto à sua auto-biografia literária, acho que v. a deve publicar. Creio que ajudaria muito a todo o mundo no Brasil se os poetas descrevessem suas experiências. [...] Quando V. tiver a sua passada a limpo, gostaria de ver uma cópia. (letter from Marseille, dated 16 June 1959)

> [As far as your idea for a literary autobiography is concerned, I believe you have to publish it. In Brazil, I believe it would be very helpful if poets themselves described their experiences. When you have your biography ready, I would like to see a copy.]

In the exchange of letters between the two poets (one nineteen years older than the other, and a clear influence on the younger poet at the start of his career), their mutual admiration comes across clearly. Mendes's early influence on Cabral is widely acknowledged in critical literature. Upon first arriving in Rio from his native Recife, in 1940, Cabral arranged to meet Murilo, who recorded the meeting in an article published in March of that same year in a journal entitled *Dom Casmurro*:

> E hoje aparece-nos, vindo pelo último navio de Recife, o poeta de vinte anos João Cabral de Melo Neto. É um poeta sem cor local [...]. No plano propriamente literário, as influências que ele mais acusa são as de Bandeira e Drummond, portanto está acertando o caminho.[1]

> [And today the twenty-year-old poet João Cabral de Melo Neto turned up, just off the boat from Recife. He is a poet who lacks local colour [...]. On a literary level, his most obvious influences are Bandeira and Drummond, so he's on the right track.]

Many years later, in a still unpublished article that he wrote about Cabral, Mendes would begin by referring to this same episode, which he would subsequently revisit repeatedly:

> Ele chegou um dia à minha casa no Rio de Janeiro: um jovem magro, seco, de palavras exatas. Completara vinte anos de idade. Queria conhecer o poeta já maduro, que adivinhou estar diante de *alguém*. ('João Cabral de Melo Neto e a poesia física')

> [He arrived at my house in Rio de Janeiro: a thin young man, of few words, to the point. He had just turned twenty. He wanted to meet the older poet, who guessed he was looking at *somebody*.]

\* \* \* \* \*

The first part of the poem 'Murilograma João Cabral de Melo Neto' (poem dated Rome, 1964, and published in the book *Convergência*, 1970) is constructed on an enunciative alternation: Mendes positions himself in relation to Cabral through a series of similarities and differences. The opening lapidary lines inscribed this relationship by highlighting a shared identification with place: 'Comigo e contigo Brasil. | Comigo e contigo Espanha' [With me and you, Brazil. | With me and you, Spain].[2]

Later, their shared connection with Andalusia is referred to: 'Comigo e contigo o Andalu, | Flamenco, Écija, los toros' [With me and you the Andalu, | Flamenco, Ecija, the bulls]. And, in the final section, we find precisely a reference to the times they spent together:

> Comigo e contigo a antibomba,
> A flor azulbranca da paz
>
> Nascida de fértil convívio
> & ritmo alternado recíproco. (Mendes, p. 691)

---

[1] In Zila Mamede, *Civil geometria: bibliografia crítica, analítica e anotada de João Cabral de Melo Neto, 1942–1982* (São Paulo: Nobel, Edusp, INL, Vitae, Governo do Estado do Rio Grande do Norte, 1987), p. 220.
[2] Murilo Mendes, *Poesia completa e prosa*, ed. by Luciana Stegagno Picchio (Rio de Janeiro: Nova Aguilar, 1994), p. 691.

[With me and you the antibomb. | The blue-white flower of peace | Born of the fertile conviviality | and reciprocal alternate rhythm.]

One could say that the second part of 'Murilograma' (portrait of the poet) is a kind of poetically condensed version of what Mendes (an extraordinary connoisseur of the work of Cabral) was writing about regarding Cabral's poetry in his correspondence to him, in which he commented on individual poems and books. Recurrent stylistic features in Mendes's work — concentration and expansion — are evident here too. On one hand, the poem ('murilograma'), on the other prose (letters; essay). This process would eventually materialize most poignantly in two of his books, which were evidently intended to complement each other, as the titles themselves suggest — from the poetry of *Tempo espanhol* (1959) (synthesis) to the prose of *Espaço espanhol* (1975) (expansion).[3]

In a letter dated 23 March 1960, after informing Mendes of the publication of his collection *Quaderna* in Portugal and of the setbacks to the intended publication of this book in Brazil, Cabral alludes to the fact that, despite experiencing similar problems in their literary lives, they differed in their relationship to poetic practice:

> Sei que v. passou pelas mesmas coisas e conseguiu sobreviver a todas as baratezas da vida literária brasileira. Mas eu sinto que nosso caso é diferente. Escrever poesia, imagino, é uma coisa sem a qual v. não poderia viver. Ao passo que para mim, é um programa, é uma coisa que resolvo fazer. Posso perfeitamente passar sem ela. Em v., a poesia completa sua vida. Dá sentido e equilíbrio a ela. Em mim não: me desequilibra.
>
> [I know that you have been through the same things and managed to survive all the challenges posed by the literary world in Brazil. Yet, I feel that my case is different. Writing poetry, I imagine, is something without which you could not live. Whereas for me, it's a plan, something I decide to do. I can perfectly do without it. For you, poetry completes your life. It gives meaning and balance to it. Not for me: it unsettles me.]

What remained unsaid was that the imbalance is actually a structural one in Cabral's work.

The correspondence between the two authors allows us to reconstruct part of many literary conversations which focused especially on poetry.[4] Mendes referred to these conversations when writing to another fellow author, Lêdo Ivo:

> Em Sevilha, durante as férias, estivemos cinco dias em casa de João e Stella, conversando poesia de manhã à noite, aproveitando também a ocasião para magníficas excursões na Andaluzia. Submeti ao João o texto do meu livro

---

[3] On the Spain of João Cabral and Murilo Mendes, see the study by Ricardo Souza Carvalho, *A Espanha de João Cabral e Murilo Mendes* (São Paulo: Editora 34, 2011).
[4] This connection was noted by José Castello in the book he published as result of a series of interviews with Cabral, carried out in 1991: *João Cabral de Melo Neto: o homem sem alma; Diário de tudo* (Rio de Janeiro: Bertrand Brasil, 2006), p. 68.

Tempo Espanhol (uns 60 poemas em que trabalhei muito), que talvez dê agora por terminado.[5] (Rome, 15 December 1958)

[In Seville, during the holidays, we spent five days at João and Stella's [Cabral and his wife's], talking about poetry from morning to night, also taking the opportunity to make wonderful trips around Andalusia. I showed João the manuscript of my book *Tempo espanhol* (some 60 poems on which I had worked extensively), which maybe I now consider finished.]

## Literary and Private Conversations

In the epistolary exchanges between the two poets one underlying presupposition is evident: the time of writing poetry is the slow time of careful vigilance; time for letter writing is what is left over, a substitute for personal conversations. In the letters, the tone we find is more off-guard, close to what we find in many of the interviews Cabral gave (a kind of 'talking-writing'), although in both the poets' letters we come across moments of more elaborate reflection, akin to critical essays.

Cabral's correspondence reveals a more-or-less latent tension between the open desire to exchange ideas (in the form of literary conversations and more public debates) and his misanthropic withdrawal from the literary scene, as we see in a letter written upon his arrival in Marseille:

Será que v. conhece aqui em Marselha alguém que valha a pena conhecer e a quem me possa apresentar? Às vezes tenho necessidade de uma conversa literária qualquer e para isso é preciso conhecer algum 'literary gentleman'. (letter of 2 November 1958)

[Do you know anyone here in Marseille worth knowing that you could introduce me to? Sometimes I feel the need to talk about literature and for this one needs to know some 'literary gentleman'.]

Or, in Madrid, when he referred to a visit to his psychiatrist, mentioned in a letter of 10 March 1961:

Estou saindo agora para o Lopez Ibor, meu psiquiatra. Estou alarmadíssimo com a minha crescente misantropia. Fujo de todo o mundo, passo dias enterrado em casa, nem respondo ao telefone. Creio que a perspectiva de ver a tanta gente conhecida é o que mais me esfria o entusiasmo que deveria estar sentindo pela volta ao Brasil.

[I am going out now to see Lopez Ibor, my psychiatrist. I am very alarmed by my increasing misanthropy. I avoid everybody, spend my days buried indoors, without even answering the phone. I believe the prospect of seeing so many familiar faces is what most dampens the enthusiasm I should be feeling in relation to my return to Brazil.]

In later statements, Cabral would quote the name of this renowned psychiatrist who, according to him, is the figure evoked in the collection *Crime na calle*

---

[5] *E agora adeus: correspondência para Lêdo Ivo* (São Paulo: Instituto Moreira Salles, 2007), p. 117.

*Relator* (1985) in one of the poems of Spanish theme, 'O exorcismo' ('Madrid, novecentos e sessenta. | Aconselham-me o Grão-Doutor' [Madrid, nineteen sixty. | They recommend the Great Doctor]).[6]

Literary and cultural exchanges between these two poets are also revealed in their correspondence, and inevitably Spain and Spanish references occupy a privileged place. In the 1948 letter which Mendes sent his friend in Barcelona (Cabral's first posting abroad with the diplomatic service) he starts a dialogue with a view to exchanging favours. In this letter, he asks for one or two books by the Spanish poet Vicente Aleixandre (1898–1984), mentioning some titles and offering in return to send Cabral books from Brazil: 'Já tenho pedido aos livreiros para fazerem vir as obras de Aleixandre; mas em vão' [I have already asked bookshops to have Aleixandre's works sent; but in vain].

Some eleven years later, the name of Aleixandre (to whom Mendes would dedicate the poem 'Sevilha', of *Tempo espanhol*, and whom he would mention in *Espaço espanhol*, as he recalled a visit he paid him) would turn up again. In a humorous reply to a question posed by Mendes, Cabral would refer to his difficulty in defining the political allegiances of the author of *Espadas como lábios*:

> O que Aleixandre deve ser é um 'cauteloso pouco a pouco', como dizia Mário de Andrade, ou 'um pezinho na frente um pezinho atrás', como diz minha tia Ester. (Letter of 4 March 1959)
>
> [What Aleixandre must be is 'gradually cautious', as Mário de Andrade used to say, or 'one step forward and one backwards', as my Aunt Ester says.]

The dialogue between Mendes and Cabral is thus based on an openness towards sharing information, details of authors, poems, sending books.

That said, reading suggestions from Cabral are rarer (at least as evidenced in the surviving letters sent to Mendes), although we find some obsessive returning to familiar literary references. At forty, Cabral is a deeply mature poet, with clear ideas in relation to poetic affinities, such as that for Marianne Moore. In a letter written in Madrid, on 23 May 1962, he wrote: 'Li hoje uma entrevista de Marianne Moore cujo fim me lembrou de V. Vou copiar o trecho para que V. a leia' [Today I read an interview with Marianne Moore, the ending of which reminded me of you. I'll copy the extract so you can read it]. At the beginning of the following month, on 6 June, Cabral sent Mendes the quotation by Moore:

> 'I think he (William Carlos Williams) wouldn't make so much of the great American language if he were plausible; or tractable. That is the beauty of it; he is willing to be reckless; if you can't be that, what's the point of the whole thing?'
>
> — Lembro a V. que M. Moore tem oitenta e tantos anos e W. C. Williams um ano mais que ela. Como se vê, os brasileiros é que ficam conformistas cedo.

---

[6] João Cabral de Melo Neto, *Obra completa* (Rio de Janeiro: Nova Aguilar, 1994), p. 596.

[Remember that M. Moore is eighty-something years old and W. C. Williams a year older than her. As you can see, Brazilians become conformists early.]

One can identify here a central and fundamental issue regarding Cabral: the unconditional and constant search for new paths to tread. One of the most interesting indications of his receptivity to Mendes's suggestions relates to the work of Francis Ponge. In a letter dated 9 February 1962, Mendes talks of the publication of Ponge's work in three volumes, by Gallimard, under the title *Le grand recueil*, which he had ordered and just received from Paris: 'E como me parece que você tem muitas afinidades com ele — já lho disse uma vez em Madrid — aqui lhe deixo a indicação' [And as I believe there are many similarities between your work and his — as I once told you in Madrid — I'm passing on the reference].

The enthusiasm with which Cabral immediately replies, in a letter sent ten days later (19 February 1962), contrasts clearly with the lack of reply to the many other suggestions, especially those related to Italian poets. Indeed, in one of his letters Cabral makes the point of declaring himself an 'anti-Italian poet'. Noteworthy is the way in which Cabral dwells on Ponge's poetry, as he awaits the books he has ordered:

> Muito obrigado pela notícia sobre a publicação dos livros completos de Ponge. Escrevi imediatamente a Paris pedindo-o. Aguardo o correio com a maior impaciência. O título que ele escolheu é ótimo, não acha? Realmente tenho muitas afinidades com ele e lamento só tê-lo lido tardíssimo. Sobretudo pela impessoalidade, pela frieza e pela engenhosidade. [...] ele é impessoal por não se contar diretamente, e com isso me identifico. Mas ao escrever atas de seus poemas, ele deixa de ser impessoal, e embora não fale do homem Ponge, mostra meio impudicamente o poeta Ponge em ato. (A isso, os *Proêmes*, *L'Araignée*, *Des cristaux naturels* são exceções.)

> [Thank you very much for the news of the publication of Ponge's complete works. I wrote to Paris immediately to order them. Very impatient as I look out for the post. The title he chose is great, don't you agree? Indeed, I have many points of contact with his work and I am sorry to have read him so late. Mainly for the impersonal, detached tone and the inventiveness. [...] he is impersonal for not speaking about himself directly, and I identify with this. But in writing on his poems, he ceases to be impersonal, and despite not speaking of Ponge the man, he reveals Ponge the poet in action. (*Proêmes*, *L'Araignée*, *Des cristaux naturels* are exceptions to this.)

Cabral's reflections on his poetics appear with some regularity in his letters. As an author who fiercely tried to erase traces of the self from his writing, and who insisted on giving a privileged place to impersonality, he expressed himself in his letter-writing, as, incidentally, he also did in interviews. But, just as in his poems, in the letters too what is particularly noteworthy is how we gain insight into his writing just as he speaks of the poetic practice of others with whom he identifies. We might recall precisely the presence of Marianne Moore and

Francis Ponge and how he identifies with these poets in *Serial* (1961), and in later allusions both in the collections in *Museu de tudo* (1975) and in *Agrestes* (1985).

The correspondence also provides insight into his candid reflections on the Brazilian poetic landscape, always with reference to his own clear conceptualizations of poetry. Under the banner of his proclaimed anti-lyricism (against any sentimentality) Cabral writes the following, in the same letter in which he reflects on Ponge's poetics: 'A morte do nosso Portinari andou inspirando a nossos amigos Carlos e Vinicius as "couves meditabundas" e as "sentimentais cenouras" que às vezes cometem' [The death of Portinari has inspired our friends Carlos and Vinicius to write the 'meditative cabbages' and 'sentimental carrots' which they sometimes commit].[7]

### Conversations on Poetic Practice: The Case of *Quaderna*

*Quaderna* (1960) was dedicated to Mendes. In his book *João Cabral de Melo Neto: o homem sem alma*, José Castello, who also wrote a biography of Vinicius de Moraes, reveals a conversation between Cabral and Vinicius in which the latter observed how Cabral's poetry was 'um longo monólogo masculino' [one long male monologue], a poetry where only men featured. Responding to this, the author of *O cão sem plumas* argued against the confessional and sentimental nature of poetry which typically defined the poetic celebration of women. Castello writes:

> Mas o comentário de Vinicius não lhe sai mais da cabeça. Nasce *Quaderna*, para pôr a mulher em cena. O livro, em ato de flagrante injustiça, pois talvez não viesse a existir sem o comentário de Vinicius, é dedicado a Murilo Mendes.[8]
>
> [But Vinicius's comment stuck. Thus, *Quaderna* was written, to put the female figure on the scene. The book, in an act of blatant injustice, since it might never have existed without Vinicius's comment, is dedicated to Murilo Mendes.]

Yet, we note how the correspondence between Cabral and Murilo reveals the complexity behind the writing of a book; in Cabral's case the extremely slow (carefully thought-out) process of composition. We discover that in 1957 Cabral had already sent Mendes a poem which would eventually be included in *Quaderna*, 'Poema(s) da cabra'. Mendes comments on this poem in a letter sent on 27 May, and on 25 September of that same year he acknowledges receipt of a group of poems ready to be published in a collection under the title *Vários poemas*:

> Fico muito feliz em saber que essas páginas exemplares me serão dedicadas. Tal dedicatória abre mais um capítulo na nossa já longa amizade, amizade que vem se ampliando através do tempo, e que considero preciosa para

---

[7] Cabral is referring to the modernist artist Candido Portinari (1903–1962) and to fellow poets Carlos Drummond de Andrade (1902–1987) and Vinicius de Moraes (1913–1980).
[8] Castello, pp. 108–09.

mim. E contribui também para que se combata essa tolice da divisão do espírito em gerações.

[I am very happy to know that these exemplary pages will be dedicated to me. This dedication opens one more chapter in our long friendship, which has grown over time and which is precious to me. And it contributes to counteract the ridiculous sense of division between generations.]

Cabral's letters reveal aspects of the book's development over the course of three years. In 1956 *Duas águas* was published, bringing together all his poetry written thus far and including three new works: *Morte e vida severina*, *Paisagens com figuras* and *Uma faca só lâmina*. The year 1957 would introduce a new phase in his career, with *Quaderna* representing a turning point in his writing. It is the work about which we find the highest number of letters, which allows us to retrieve important information on its composition.[9] In early February 1958, Cabral sends his fellow poet some significant information:

> Sobre nosso livro: o Aloísio Magalhães levou há meses para o Recife os poemas que v. conhece.[10] Andei hesitando se devia ou não publicar, etc., etc. Afinal resolvi-me. Terminei mais 2, 'Paisagens com cupim' e 'Sevilha', e dei o imprima-se que o Aloísio pedia. Assim, creio que breve sairá. Mudei de nome: chama-se agora Quaderna mas está claro que a dedicatória a Murillo Mendes [sic] continua.

> [About our book: Aloísio Magalhães took copies of the poems you saw to Recife some months ago. I have been hesitating whether to publish or not, etc., etc. In the end, I've decided to go ahead. I've finished two more poems, 'Paisagens com cupim' and 'Sevilha', and I have given Aloísio the go-ahead to print. So, I think it will be out soon. I've changed the title and it's now Quaderna, but obviously the dedication to Murilo Mendes remains.]

The use of the possessive in 'nosso livro' highlights the strong ties between the poets, and a similar reference to the book appears elsewhere, including at the end of 1958, when Cabral arrived in Marseille and wrote to Mendes. This suggests that the title was still not actually definitive, but as the correspondence progresses the letters begin to refer to the collection as it indeed was entitled: *Quaderna*.

Finally, in 1960, in a letter dealing with the issue of 'Quaderna', Cabral gives some good news: 'Quaderna: saiu em Portugal. A edição do Brasil mandei suspendê-la, definitiva e irrevogavelmente' [Quaderna: published in Portugal. I have definitely and irrevocably stopped the Brazilian edition].[11] The news is

---

[9] A similar case relates to Cabral's *Psicologia da Composição* (1947), which was dedicated to Lauro Escorel. Cabral's correspondence with Lauro Escorel (held at the Arquivo-Museu da Literatura da Casa Rui Barbosa) is extremely revealing of the book's composition.
[10] Aloísio Magalhães (1927–1982), highly respected artist, illustrator and graphic designer.
[11] Worth mentioning here is a significant Portuguese connection. Two books are directly or indirectly points of contact in the dialogue between the poets: Mendes's *Tempo espanhol* was published in Portugal in 1959 (by Moraes Editores), while *Quaderna* was also published in Portugal, in 1960 (by Guimarães Editores).

accompanied by a revelation which in a sense is not surprising given the poet's obsessive pursuit of the new: the poem 'bailadora andaluza' acquires new lines and the fact that the poem should open the collection is symbolic:

> Tem duas coisas novas que v. não conhece e que só em dezembro, na Espanha, consegui acabar: são as partes 5 e 6 dos 'Estudos para uma bailadora andaluza'. A parte 5 é o resultado de uma observação sua sobre o baile flamenco. (Marseille, 23 March 1960)
>
> [There are two new parts which you haven't seen and which I only managed to complete in Spain in December: parts 5 and 6 of 'Estudos para uma bailadora andaluza'. Part 5 is the result of a comment of yours about flamenco dancing.]

After completing *Quaderna*, Cabral continues to comment on his creative process, his obsessive paring down, what he calls 'escovadela' [literally: 'a brush-up'] in one of his letters:

> Ando ocupado com a instalação do novo apartamento. É enorme e me sinto perdido. Mas estou aproveitando a novidade do ambiente para me forçar a escrever um pouco. Estou passando a limpo as coisas quase feitas para que depois possa dar nelas uma escovadela final. (Madrid, 1 August 1960)
>
> [I have been busy with setting up our new flat. It is huge and I feel lost in it. But I am taking advantage of the new space to force myself to write a little. I am tidying up some material which is nearly ready for its final brush-up.]

In 1962, he acknowledges his friend's role in helping him look at Seville as a feminine city, a defining feature of his later works: 'Sevilha: V. acha bem, dizendo que Sevilha é a cidade mais mulher que V. conhece. [...] Se não é a mais mulher é a que melhor corresponde ao tipo de mulher que me interessa' [Seville: you are right when you say that Seville is the most feminine city you know. [...] If it's not the most feminine, it is the one that comes closest to the type of woman that interests me] (Seville, 8 August 1962).

Five years earlier, in the letter of 25 September 1957 mentioned above, Mendes highlighted the representation of women as the distinguishing feature of Cabral's work: 'Você consegue, sem "cantar", sem dó de peito, alargar a zona da sua poética, conferindo às imagens ligadas à mulher a sua dignidade antiga' [You manage to broaden your poetic landscape without 'singing', without heartache, by restoring an ancient dignity to your images of women].

Indeed, *Quaderna*'s poem 'Estudos para uma bailadora andaluza' is key in inaugurating a new phase, in which the female figure will prove a recurring feature. In the poem, the succession of similes (fire, horse, telegraphy, book, statue, ear of corn) follow on from each other in pursuit of intensity, of the 'extreme'; the image of fire establishes the tone of this radical search, free of commonplaces. Fire will appear again in a similar process of association in *A educação pela pedra* (1966), in a poem about two flamenco dancers, Fernanda and Bernarda de Utrera.

## Flamenco and the 'bailadoras'

Cabral's second period in Spain (Seville) would be characterized by his enthusiasm for flamenco. In a letter sent to Mendes in 1957, Cabral speaks of his new-found fascination which replaced his earlier one for bulls and bullfighting: 'é realmente algo de fabuloso e não creio que exista em nenhum outro lugar uma manifestação de arte popular da altura do cante espanhol' [it is truly fabulous and I believe nowhere else is there popular art that matches the Spanish flamenco song] (Seville, 14 February 1957).

In 1957, Mendes had replied to Cabral as he followed the latter's enthusiasm in his research on flamenco: 'Pelo pouco que conheço do cante flamenco, avalio o prazer que v. está agora tendo em aprofundá-lo. É sem dúvida uma grande coisa e das mais reveladoras da qualidade funda da España' [From the little I know about flamenco song, I can appreciate the pleasure you are gaining from learning more about it. It is without doubt a great thing and among the most revealing of Spain's deeper qualities] (27 May 1957). Immediately following this letter, Mendes asks his friend to suggest 'um bom disco long-play do flamenco' [a good flamenco LP]. In a *post-scriptum* to a 25 September letter of that same year, Mendes would insist again, and at every stage he declares his desire to understand Spain better. In the above-mentioned September letter, Mendes refers to some Brazilians passing through Madrid (they are Ramiro Martins and Murilo Rubião) as the best way of getting hold of the records and says that, despite not usually wishing to bother others, 'quando se trata de Espanha, perco a vergonha' [when it's about Spain then I lose all shame]. And again: at the end of a letter dated 27 May we find an underlined request by Mendes: 'Adeus, meu caro. Escreva-me logo que puder. Mande-me algo seu sobre España [Farewell, my friend. Write as soon as you can. Send me something you've written on Spain].

The poem 'Estudos para uma bailadora andaluza' occupies a significant place in Cabral's *oeuvre* given it is the first of a number of poems which would invoke the figure of the flamenco dancer. Some of these figures appear in the titles of the poems, such as Carmen Amaya, of Triana, the sisters Bernarda and Fernanda de Utrera, or the Niña de los Peines.

In 1959, Cabral wrote to Mendes from Marseille to discuss the trip of a dancer to Rome. Carmen Carrera was the first name suggested. The contact was not made directly as would happen later in relation to the trip by Trini España. In a letter dated 13 October, Cabral acknowledges his role as intermediary in this process: a Spanish poet friend of his had passed through Marseille and Cabral had asked him to contact Carmen Carrera, in Seville. Cabral waits for news for a month, then on 23 November he writes again saying he still has no concrete news regarding Carmen Carrera's trip to Rome. There had been some miscommunication, because she had sent Cabral a postcard from Madrid and he was left in some doubt as to whether the dancer was actually in Seville, as he thought, which might have explained why the above-mentioned poet, Aquilino

Duque, had not been able to contact her. Cabral states he is waiting for a reply from Carmen Carrera to a letter he himself had sent her to a Madrid address. He adds that as soon as he is in Madrid he will also deal with the issue personally.

How might we interpret these exchanges? Cabral, spending time with dancers, dealing with them and trying to support them. From the letters, we can piece together some elements related to these contacts. Indeed, one can observe how the poet, usually so restrained, and always claiming to be a bad letter-writer, reveals some extraordinary effort in dealing with practical issues related to the dancer's visit to Rome.

At the beginning of the following year, Cabral moved to Spain, a significant move within the poet's trajectory. As he tells Mendes in a letter sent from Seville, on 14 January 1960, the prospect of an imminent diplomatic posting to the Embassy of Brazil in Buenos Aires prompted him to make the trip to Spain: 'quis me despedir do que realmente me importa' [I wanted to say goodbye to what really matters to me.] Before reaching Seville he had been in Madrid: 'Fiquei em Madrid mais tempo do que pensava, fartando-me de flamenco — que, no inverno anda melhor por lá do que por aqui' [I stayed in Madrid longer than I expected, enjoying loads of flamenco — which in the winter is better there than it is here].

The tension between impersonal expression, which the poet purported to aim for, and the way in which his personal experiences find their way in between the lines of his writing is central to his work. Without wishing to engage in a reading of his work through a biographical lens, one cannot fail to underline the fact that flamenco and all things Andalusian in his work are linked to his real-life experiences.

## Muse

In a letter of 1 August 1960 the name of the dancer Trini España appears once again, albeit in a simple reference: 'Vs. não têm o que agradecer: o prazer foi meu. Trini España segue dançando como sempre e mesmo sem mim vocês teriam ouvido falar dela' [You do not need to thank me: my pleasure. Trini España is still dancing, and even without me you would have heard of her]. Trini would be referenced again two years later, in 1962. Then, Cabral would pick up on the issue discussed in the letters sent from Madrid at the end of 1959 (in which he suggested the possibility of Carmen Carrera going to Rome) and writes to Mendes with a new proposal. The poet's involvement with the issue comes across strongly in all the letters that deal with the project. In a letter sent from Madrid, on 5 April, Cabral speaks of Trini as the most accomplished of dancers:

> Agora estou escrevendo para perguntar se aquele seu amigo daí, do grupo de teatro que queria ver dançar a Carmen Carrera, ainda está interessado em flamenco. Creio que a Trini España, que está num ponto realmente excepcional de sua carreira, poderia, melhor que ninguém (fora

Carmen Amaya) dar a eles uma boa demonstração. Faço a proposta com consentimento dela, que gostaria de sair um pouco da Espanha, para variar. Ela levaria um guitarrista e um bom cantador, e nos intervalos de cada número de dança, estes fariam números isolados (ou mais gente, se daí preferirem). Se V. puder fazer alguma coisa peço dizer-me.

[I am now writing to ask whether your friend there, of the theatre group who wanted to see Carmen Carrera dance, is still interested in flamenco. I believe Trini España, who is at an exceptional stage in her career, could, better than anyone (bar Carmen Amaya) give them a good demonstration. I am suggesting this with her consent, as she would like to travel outside of Spain, for a change. She would take a guitarist and a good singer with her, and in the intervals between dances they would do some individual numbers (or together, if you prefer that). If you are able to arrange something, please let me know.]

From then on, we find several letters in which Cabral deals with the topic. He is absolutely Trini's agent. In letters from Madrid, from 16 and 23 May, he thanks Mendes for his assistance in dealing with a friend of his working at the Teatro Club and explains what negotiations he is engaged in (payments, portfolio, photographs etc.). Later, in letters from Seville, dated 8 August and 15 October, accounts are mentioned again, alongside queries regarding change of dates. In a December letter, Cabral thanks Mendes for his support, sorry that the Trini España venture did not succeed.

But the letter dated 8 August deserves particular attention. The tone with which it opens differs from the others, in which he often refers to the difficulty in writing. Following the upheaval of settling into the consulate in Seville, he finds a moment to write, saying; 'Só hoje posso arranjar um pouco de tempo para carta de prazer' [Only today have I managed to find a little time to write a letter for pleasure]. Here is the section in which Trini España is mentioned:

> Trini España está em San Sebastián. Foi para lá no dia 3 e assim ainda a vi uns dias na Venta Real. Segue superior, talvez até 'Más hecha, si puede'. É uma lástima que o êxito material de artistas deste ramo esteja tão sujeito à comercialização. Penso muitas vezes que a poesia é a arte mais feliz de todas, porque a mais independente. Se ninguém nos edita, se ninguém nos lê, há sempre a possibilidade de fazer duas ou três cópias de um poema e soltar por aí. E o poeta — diferentemente da bailadora, pode viver de outra coisa: instalando consulados, por exemplo. Depois de quase seis meses, senti quanto minha poesia posterior a 1956 (que foi quando vim para Sevilha e a vi dançar pela primeira vez) deve à arte dela. V. talvez não compreenda: mas eu sinto que escrevo agora muito mais 'por derecho', com 'los pies más claros', 'exponiendo más', 'aguantando más', etc. veja por exemplo como desde *Quaderna* o que eu faço é menos cantante. As exceções, em *Quaderna*, são os 'Jogos frutais' e a 'Estrada de Caxangá' que vieram escritos do Brasil. Pois eu, até então, embora me enjoassem os dois perigos da 'tradição' luso-brasileira (que é o oratório e o cantante, Castro Alves e o lundu) achava que uma certa dose de 'jingle' era indispensável (há cantante até numa faca só lâmina). Quando eu vi que era possível na

dança se eliminar o 'jingle', isto é, até na dança, arte que me parece mais dependente da música, compreendi que na poesia seria possível, também. Daí essa abordagem prosaica do assunto do poema que só de 1956 para cá emprego sem nenhum receio.

Bom, meu caro Murilo: não sei porque me estendi dessa maneira em minudências de cozinha literária que não interessam a ninguém. Talvez seja a ausência de gente a quem falar disso e o tempo que levo sem fazê-lo. Desculpe. Volto à sua carta.

[Trini España is in San Sebastian. She left on the 3rd and I therefore saw her for a few days in Venta Real. She is still exceptional, perhaps even more accomplished, if that's possible. It is a shame that the success of these artists should be vulnerable to commercial pressures. I often think how poetry is the most fortunate of the arts, because it is the most independent. If no one publishes us, if nobody reads us, there is always the possibility of making two, three copies of a poem and distributing it around. And the poet — unlike the dancer — can make a living from other things: setting up consulates, for example. After nearly six months, I felt how much my poetry post-1956 (which was when I came to Seville and saw her dance for the first time) owes much to her art. Perhaps you do not understand: but I feel that I write now much more 'directly', with 'clearer feet', 'expressing more', 'carrying more', etc. See how, for example, since *Quaderna* what I do is less musical. Exceptions in *Quaderna* are 'Jogos frutais' and 'Estrada de Caxangá', which were written in Brazil. Because I, until then, despite abhorring the two pitfalls of the Luso-Brazilian 'tradition' (the preaching and the singing, Castro Alves and lundu) thought that a certain dose of 'jingle' was indispensable (there is song even in *Uma faca só lâmina*). When I realized that it was possible to eliminate the 'jingle' from dance, i.e. even from dance, which seems to me the art that most depends on music, it dawned on me that it would be possible to do the same in poetry. Hence, this prosaic approach to poetry which I have adopted since 1956 without fear.

Well, my dear Murilo: I don't quite know why I have gone on in this way with minor concerns from the literary kitchen which interest nobody. Maybe it is the absence of people with whom to speak about this and the time I spend without doing it. My apologies. I go back to your letter.]

This extract is central to understanding Cabral's perspective on flamenco and its impact on his work. What emerges from the letter to his friend is Cabral's ability to analyse, to consider critically (a defining feature of his poetry too). The extract is also significant in helping us identify the place of *Quaderna* and of Trini España within his *oeuvre* as a whole (even though this dancer is never mentioned explicitly in the poems, unlike other dancers). It reveals the contribution of this popular art form to the development of Cabral's poetics. Features such as its 'visual syntax' (the rigorous organization of poems, for example) or the rhythm of his lines, from *Quaderna* onwards largely stem from his knowledge of and contact with the art of flamenco.

## Mutual Commentators

Among Mendes's comments on Cabral's poetry we find in their correspondence, I wish to highlight two lines of argument: his emphatic support for his writing, not hesitating to speak of masterpieces and brilliance in relation to much of what he read; his obvious rejection of commonplace comments, such as the much referred to 'dryness' of Cabral's poetry, to which Mendes prefers 'humanity'. See, in this respect, a letter sent from Rome, dated 29 May 1960:

> Espero que tenha recebido minha carta de 6, agradecendo-lhe QUADERNA. É possível que eu seja suspeito, mas quanto mais releio o livro, mais fabuloso o acho. E não só pelo seu aspecto técnico — mas também pela sua profunda humanidade escondida sob as espécies intelectuais. Obra de alguém que chegou a uma grande SABEDORIA.

> [I hope you received my letter dated the 6th, thanking you for sending *Quaderna*. I am possibly biased, but the more I read the book the more wonderful I find it. And not only in terms of technique — but also for its deep humanity, disguised under intellectual virtuosity. The work of someone who has acquired great wisdom.]

The poets follow one another's literary careers with great interest, even if sometimes at different paces. From the promise of a study on Mendes by Cabral which never materialized, to the text that Mendes wrote on Cabral (unpublished), the terms of their dialogue were defined and their mutual support saw them navigate the narrow logic of the publishing world. If Mendes's letters engaged at length with Cabral's books, Cabral in turn did so with less regularity but was always accurate in his letters and above all always 'pessoalíssimo' [very personal], that is, writing in his own voice, projecting his own understanding of poetry onto his comments on Mendes's writing.

What, then, makes this dialogue between Mendes and Cabral so unique? Certainly, who they are, but above all the obstinate search around which their dialogue develops: their strong belief in the creation of a poetic space, visualized through powerful imagery. Even before knowing the place, both poets were already making connections, as though Spain were the necessary name for an invented land.

In different ways, both poets carried Spain inside them, even before experiencing it, even before setting foot there. This was clearly the case with Mendes, whose engagement with the country involved a strong degree of idealization. Yet, the imagined land is not always a simple metaphor. What moves these poets is not, then, a mere rhetorical drive, but a sense of belonging.

The distance from their native land would serve to accelerate the process of transition from sign to metaphor. The dark roots of the real Brazil would be more intensely and painfully perceived at a distance. This is evidenced in the letters they exchanged. And it is behind the genesis of Cabral's *Cão sem plumas*

(1950) and Mendes's *Tempo espanhol* (1959). Spain is Brazil. In their adopted land the link between earth and poetry became clearer. And it is when they recognized themselves in the name (another land, yet the same) and made it familiar that the poets began their dialogue. Under the sign of Spain they came together, in a shared experience. Their exchange of letters captures fragments, chapters of this relationship, from its beginning. The largest number of letters are clustered around the period of the composition of *Quaderna*. Beside this, many other moments: of celebrations, of expected visits, following each other's readings, justifying decisions taken. Nearly always, Cabral's voice comes out strongest (his assessments, his pessimism), articulating strong opinions, but in a measured and grateful tone. Mendes's tone is more subdued, meticulous and patient, critical, voracious and present. Beyond the pettiness of everyday experience, beyond the tribulations of so-called literary life and the worries life threw at them, above all else, there remained two different personalities converging in poetic understanding.

*Translated by Sara Brandellero*

I wish to thank Murilo Mendes's widow, Maria da Saudade Cortesão Mendes, who in 2009 allowed me to publicize Cabral's letters and Murilo Mendes's unpublished study entitled: 'João Cabral de Melo Neto ou a poesia física'. I am especially grateful to João Nuno Morais Alçada, who gave me access to the texts through photocopies. Thank you also to Inês Cabral and to Eduardo Coelho, who put me in contact with her and who was at the time director of the museum archive Casa de Rui Barbosa, in Rio de Janeiro, thus allowing me to consult Cabral's archive. This article stems from a paper presented at the symposium 'João Cabral de Melo Neto and his Transnational Legacy: Dialogues and Confluences', Canning House, London, 9 October 2009. I thank David Treece and Sara Brandellero wholeheartedly for the invitation, and the exchanges it generated. I thank Sara Brandellero in particular for the translation of my article.

# *Auto do frade* by João Cabral de Melo Neto: A Trope of the Passion

Vinicius Mariano de Carvalho

*King's College London*

'Quem bebe da minha caneca tem sede de liberdade'
[whoso drinketh of my cup shall thirst for freedom]
Frei Caneca[1]

## Introduction

The interpretation proposed in this article of the one-act play, *Auto do frade* (1984) by João Cabral de Melo Neto, seeks to address this work under a hermeneutical bias which would allow us to interpret it as a trope of the Passion of the Christ, from its formal aspect to its deeply significant exegetical elements that relate it to another earlier work of his, also of a somewhat religious nature, his first one-act play *Morte e vida severina* (1956).

The comparison of *Auto do frade* to the Passion of the Christ is not original on my part. Arnaldo Saraiva, in an article entitled 'O *Auto do frade* de João Cabral: a velha e a nova história', states that 'o *Auto do frade* é um verdadeiro auto da paixão, dividido em estações que constituem a metade da via-sacra' [*Auto do frade* is a true act of passion, divided into stations that make up half of the Way of the Cross].[2] However, the author does not develop this interpretation in the text, leaving us only with the title. Another much deeper study about this trope is that by Sara Brandellero in the second chapter of her book *On a Knife-Edge: The Poetry of João Cabral de Melo Neto* (2011). In this chapter, Brandellero more properly exposes the elements of this poem that allow it to be read in parallel with the Passion of the Christ. For Brandellero, 'True enough, many of the elements of the story of the Passion found their way into Cabral's second *auto*.'[3]

For this analysis of *Auto do frade* as a trope of the Passion, I will first note some aspects of the charisma of the Order of the Carmelites, of which Frei

---

[1] All translations are by the author, unless otherwise stated.
[2] Arnaldo Saraiva, 'O "Auto do frade" de João Cabral: a velha e a nova história', in *Literatura e História: actas do Colóquio Internacional*, ed. by Maria de Fátima Marinho and Francisco Topa, vol. II (Porto: Departamento de Estudos Portugueses e Estudos Românicos da Faculdade de Letras do Porto, 2004), pp. 225–30 (p. 229).
[3] Sara Brandellero, *On a Knife-Edge: The Poetry of João Cabral de Melo Neto* (Oxford: Oxford University Press, 2011), p. 58.

Caneca was a member, and identify which elements of mysticism and spirituality of this Order around the Passion are reflected in Cabral's play. I will then focus on the seven moments in which Frei Caneca speaks in the play, in parallel to the seven last utterances, or 'words', of Christ on the cross. In doing so, I wish to show how Cabral, in a way, completes a story of salvation, which began in *Morte e vida severina*. This reading may bring to light other interpretations for the end of the play, by putting it in a theological perspective — not one from an orthodox theology, perhaps, but a theology as developed by Cabral, a theology of drought and Pernambuco, a theology of hope and freedom.

## *Auto do frade* and the Friar in the *auto*

Composed between 1981 and 1983, but only published in 1984, *Auto do frade* is often listed as another dramatic poem by João Cabral, along with *Morte e vida severina* (written 1954–55). In fact, there are several parallels in terms of form and also in content (although this may not seem initially obvious). *Morte e vida severina* features the subtitle of *Auto de natal pernambucano* [Christmas Auto in Pernambuco], whereas *Auto do frade* comes under the heading of *voice poems*. That is, both works are poems intended to be performed and made public.[4]

Both dramatic poems are traditionally tied to religious *autos*, practices of medieval origin widely cultivated in Brazil since the early years of Portuguese colonization. One of the early Jesuit missionaries to Brazil, José de Anchieta (1534–1597), for example, used *autos* as a tool to convert the indigenous population. In these religious plays, more than the direct and denotative reference of religious values, it is the power of metaphor, the connotative, the allegorical that really counts in the catechetical exercise. For example, in the *Auto de São Lourenço* (1583), authored by Anchieta himself, elements such as a dialogue between St Sebastian and St Lawrence on the one hand, speaking in Portuguese, and a devil named Guaixará, a Tupi speaker, followed by speeches by allegorical figures such as 'Fear of God' and 'Love of God', are noteworthy more for their symbolic efficacy than for an argumentative plausibility. The Brazilian North-East, particularly, has always been fertile ground for the flourishing of religious *autos* that function as paraliturgies of a popular religiosity oblivious to ecclesiastical discipline. This popular religiosity truly embodies the Divine Word in the core of the people and performatively ritualizes the Passion of the Christ as a mirror of the fate of a suffering people.

In this sense, both dramatic poems by Cabral complement each other as a liturgical cycle: while *Morte e vida severina* brings to life a (messianic) boy born in the slums of Recife and enacts the promise of a new life amongst the harsh realities of migrant existence, by theologically embodying Christ in the poor child, *Auto do frade* completes the salvation story, by celebrating the passion

---

[4] With respect to this, and especially the fact that this poem was written also as a possible film script, see Brandellero, p. 52.

and (eschatological) death of a Recife native of humble background, who, through his wisdom and action, becomes a quasi-prophet among his people, to the point of disturbing the political *status quo*.

As in *Morte e vida severina*, the boy, the son of migrants, is born into the poverty of Recife, drawing a parallel with the Child of God. Frei Caneca incorporates in his life the prophetic virtues of Judaism/Christianity to denounce and announce. Like the biblical prophets (and Christ himself is described as a prophet in many passages of the Gospels), Frei Joaquim do Amor Divino Rabelo does not deny his humble origins and takes on the nickname of Caneca, in honour of his father, a cooper by profession. He accepts his chalice biblically, just as Christ does and declares he has done on the Mount of Olives before his arrest and passion. This acceptance defines his public life and inevitably leads him to his death. In the sentence that is used as the title, we can clearly see the biblical intertextuality used by the friar. By exchanging the chalice for the cup, he transmutes the image of Christ to himself and assigns himself the same messianic nature.

The historical character Frei Joaquim do Amor Divino Rabelo was born Joaquim da Silva Rabelo in Recife in 1779, but is remembered simply by the nickname Frei Caneca, a nickname adopted in honour of his father, as stated above. He professed vows in the Carmelite Order and participated in the Pernambuco Revolution, which proclaimed a republic in Recife in the year 1817. For this engagement, he was arrested and served time in Salvador until 1821. Back in Pernambuco again, he started to teach philosophy, geometry and rhetoric and began his work as a journalist and political activist through the newspaper *Typhis Pernambucano*, an agent of extreme opposition to the central government of newly independent Brazil.[5]

The opposition to the government of Emperor D. Pedro I, which went beyond pamphleteering, led to Pernambuco breaking with the central government on 2 July 1824, and the establishing a republic called the Confederation of the Equator. With no support from other provinces, however, the movement was severely suppressed, and Frei Caneca, as a leader of one of the columns of the movement, was again arrested on 29 November 1824, and sentenced to be hanged in December of the same year. Despite several requests for clemency, his execution was set for 13 January 1825. Given the refusal by various hangmen to kill him, however, his sentence was changed to death by shooting. His body was left at the gates of the Convent of the Carmelites, who collected and buried him in a place which is unknown to this very day. Overall, eleven Confederates were executed, three of them in Rio de Janeiro. Frei Caneca was the first one.

João Cabral's *auto* stages Frei Caneca's last day and does it so as to suggest by its structure a paraliturgy of the Way of the Cross, celebrated during Lent in

---

[5] All historical information referred to here was gathered from Evaldo Cabral de Mello, *Frei Joaquim do Amor Divino Caneca* (São Paulo: Editora 34, 2001). The historian Evaldo Cabral de Mello is João Cabral's brother.

Catholic communities. At the same time, it maintains formalities close to the medieval *autos* of passion, which together with Christmas *autos* (as in *Morte e vida severina*), make up the two major cycles of popular liturgical feasts. As pointed out in the introduction to this essay, the relationship between *Auto do frade* and the Passion of the Christ is not new and has already been addressed in other studies. What seems a novelty, however, is the relationship between the meaning of the Passion of the Christ to the spirituality of the Carmelite Order, of which Caneca was a member, and how João Cabral works with this meaning, particularly in the utterances of Caneca in the poem, coincidentally seven, like the number of times that Christ is reported to have spoken during the Passion.

### Frei Caneca, a Carmelite

The first members of the Order of the Blessed Virgin of Mount Carmel, known as the Carmelite Order or Carmelite friars, arrived in Brazil in the year 1580 and founded the first convent in the year 1584, in Olinda, Recife. There were only four religious members, led by Friar Bernardo Pimentel. The growth of the Order was significant, and by 1718 there were seven convents scattered mostly along the coast, from São Paulo to Olinda. In 1720 these convents formed an independent Province under the name of the Carmelite Province of St Elijah. It continued growing and the Carmelites opened houses in Maranhão and Pará. From the beginning of their pastoral activity in Brazil the Carmelites had been present and active in the political life of the country, especially during the colonial period, when Church and State were confused.[6]

The order has its mythical origins on the slopes of Mount Carmel, today in the State of Israel, where the Prophet Elijah lived. Possibly at the height of medieval devotions of the imitation of Christ, hermits started living a contemplative secluded life on this site. What is known for sure is that the year 1207 is considered as the date of the founding of the Order. That year, St Albert wrote what would be the Rule of the Carmelite Religious Life. The spiritual and practical values expressed in the rule are well defined by the title of an article for the *Toronto Journal of Theology* by Gill K. Goulding, in which she reviews the principles of the Carmelite mystique. The article is called: 'Passion, Prophecy and Perseverance: The Leitmotif of Carmel'.[7]

The fact that their origin is associated with Prophet Elijah would deeply mark the prophetic character of the Carmelite charisma and spirituality.[8] As

---

[6] Historical information about the Carmelites in Brazil is to be found on the Order's website: <http://www.carmelo.com.br/default.asp?pag=p000005> [accessed 9 May 2014].
[7] Gill K. Goulding, 'Passion, Prophecy and Perseverance: The Leitmotif of Carmel', *Toronto Journal of Theology*. 21.2 (2005), 169–82.
[8] Cf. Patrick Thomas McMahon, 'Carmelite Spirituality', online at <http://carmelstream.com/CarmelStream/In%20Depth%20Articles/CARMELITE%20SPIRITUALITY--McMahon.pdf>, p. 16 [accessed 9 May 2014].

prophets, the friars should be bridges between the Old and New Testaments, both denouncers of the oppressive structures that drove men away from the kingdom of God and announcers of this Good News kingdom. In the task of prophets, the virtue of perseverance had to be present, since it was animated by the Spirit of God. This perseverance is highlighted in the rule of St Albert:

> 18 [XIV, xvi] Since human life on earth is a trial and all who want to live devotedly in Christ suffer persecution; your enemy the devil prowls about like a roaring lion seeking whom he might devour. You must then with all diligence put on the armour of God so that you may be able to stand up to the ambushes of the enemy.[9]

The third point of this Carmelite *way of life* is passion, a theme that is present throughout the history of the Order. The imitation of Christ should be, for the friar (and the nun — in 1452, the first female Carmelite convent was opened), a subject for greater zeal: imitating the love of Christ in everything, including his passion. In the words of Fitzgerald, 'The Carmelite tradition transmits the legacy of profound passion.'[10] And more:

> The ardor of their desire to love and be transformed in love and the intensity of their experience of, reflection on and appropriation of human suffering is precisely what characterizes those marked by the Carmelite ethos.[11]

It is within this tradition and mystique that Frei Caneca is educated and it is as professor of the Carmelite Order that the friar operates in his public life. His political stance is no different from his religious practice, revealing his passion, perseverance and prophetism. João Cabral identifies these features very clearly in the Carmelite and translates them in his *auto* of the passion of the Friar, drawing a parallel with the Passion of the Christ.

Another important aspect in the life of the Carmel is the practice of silence. The rule of St Albert is quite clear on this aspect and insists on the value of silence as a practice of justice. Carmelite spirituality shall drink from this value, and the eloquence of St John of the Cross and St Teresa of Avila's mystical and negative poetry shall come out of silence. The rule states:

> 21 [XVI, xviii] The apostle therefore recommends silence, when he tells us to work in it; the prophet too testifies that silence is the promotion of justice; and again, in silence and in hope will be your strength. [...] you are to be diligent in avoiding much talking, since Scripture states and experience likewise teaches, sin is not absent where there is much talking; also he who is careless in speech will experience evil, and the one who uses many words harms his soul. Again the Lord says in the gospel: an account will have to be given on the day of judgement for every vain word. Each of

---

[9] *The Rule of Saint Albert*, trans. by Christopher O'Donnell, online at <http://www.carmelite.org/documents/Spirituality/rsacodtranslation.pdf> [accessed 9 May 2014].
[10] Constance Fitzgerald, 'Passion in the Carmelite Tradition: Edith Stein', *Spiritus: A Journal of Christian Spirituality* (Johns Hopkins University), 2.2 (Fall 2002), 217–35 (p. 217).
[11] Idem.

you is to weigh his words and have a proper restraint for his mouth, so that he may not stumble and fall through speech and his fall be irreparable and fatal. He is with the prophet to guard his ways so that he does not offend through the tongue. Silence, which is the promotion of justice, is likewise to be diligently and carefully observed.[12]

We will see how these values of perseverance, prophecy, passion and practice of silence are echoed in Frei Caneca in João Cabral's poem. Whether he was aware of the Carmelite spirituality or not, the poet from Pernambuco captured these values very well in the character of Frei Caneca.

### The Passion of Frei Caneca according to João Cabral

If we read *Auto do frade* as drawing a parallel with the Passion of the Christ, what we find structurally is that it reproduces seven stations of the Via Dolorosa, not fourteen as in the paraliturgy of the Way of the Cross. The first of them, 'In the Cell', is played out through the voices of the provincial and the jailer. In the dialogue between them, the death-and-sleep relationship is brought to the fore. Indeed, the sometimes almost surreal dialogue takes us back to the sleep of the disciples on the Mount of Olives when Christ withdraws to pray, moments before his arrest. Here, though, it is the Saint who sleeps, or at least so the provincial and the jailer think when they try to awaken him:

> — Dorme fundo como um morto.
> — Mas está vivo. Vamos ressuscitá-lo.
> — Deste sono ainda pode ser ressuscitado
> — Deste sono sim. Do outro, nem que ponham a porta abaixo.
> — Esta dormindo como um santo.
> — Santo não dorme. Os santos são é moucos. Mas têm os olhos bem abertos. Vi na igreja.[13]

> [— He sleeps deeply like a dead man.
> — But he is awake. Let's resurrect him.
> — From this sleep he can still be woken.
> — From this one, yes. From the other, not even if they kick the door down.
> — He is sleeping like a saint.
> — Saints don't sleep. Saints are deaf. But they have their eyes wide open. I saw that in church.]

This sleep–death relationship will be important throughout the poem and is referred to repeatedly in the text. Comparatively, Frei Caneca is silent in prison, like Christ in front of his accusers, refusing to defend himself or even say anything (see Gospel of Matthew 27. 11 and Mark 14. 61). Frei Caneca, as a Carmelite, practises silence as a cultivation of justice, and in silence he finds greater eloquence than in many speeches.

[12] *The Rule of Saint Albert.*
[13] João Cabral de Melo Neto, *A Escola das Facas e Auto do Frade* (Rio de Janeiro: Objetiva, 2008), pp. 109–10.

As already stated, the progress of the poem is structurally close to a Way of the Cross, narrating the way taken by the friar from prison to the place where he will be executed and his interactions with the people and power along the way, in clear allusions to Christ on his way to Calvary.

Another notable example of this parallelism is the relationship between the scene in which Frei Caneca is stripped of the holy orders by the ecclesiastical degradation ritual before being handed over to secular justice, and that of Christ being stripped of his clothing before his crucifixion (Matthew 27. 27, Mark 15, Luke 16 and 23. 34). The symbolic act of removing the Friar's sacred clothing puts him in the same condition as Christ, devoid of everything for his sacrifice. Though not deliberately, when they undress Frei Caneca, they give him more strength in persevering in the imitation of the Passion. It is important to note here that this undressing is not a departure from his communion with the Carmelite community. Frei Caneca is not being excommunicated. Indeed, according to canon law, executing a priest belonging to the Orders is itself a reason for excommunication.[14]

In our reading we would like, however, to further explore the instances when Frei Caneca speaks in João Cabral's poem and establish another parallel with the Passion of the Christ: His last words on the Cross.

The reports of the arrest, conviction and death of Christ, gathered under the title Passion of the Christ, are not in only one chronicle in the gospels. None of the four authors gives us a detailed portrait of that moment. It is necessary to compare the four canonical Gospels in order to have a general picture of this central event in the history of Christianity. In the established tradition, and again, collecting the four gospels, we came to the seven discursive moments of Christ. These 'seven words', or utterances, became central in the liturgical celebrations of the Holy Week, and an entire sermon is dedicated to them. Hundreds of musical compositions also relied on this motto or even on the words literally. The 'words' are as follows:

 1 — 'Father, forgive them, for they know not what they do' (Luke 23. 34)
 2 — 'Verily I say unto thee, today shalt thou be with me in paradise' (Luke 23. 43)
 3 — 'He said to His mother, "Woman, behold thy son!" Then He said to the disciple, "Behold thy mother!"' (John 19. 26–27)
 4 — '"Eloi, Eloi, lama sabachthani?" — which means, "My God, my God, why hast thou forsaken me?"' (Matthew 27. 46; Mark 15. 34)
 5 — 'I thirst' (John 19. 28)
 6 — 'It is finished' (John 19. 30)
 7 — 'Father, into thy hands I commend my spirit' (Luke 23. 46)

---

[14] During an interview for IHU Online, Vera Haas, when analysing the representation of Frei Caneca in the work in question, makes a mistake by asserting that 'Excommunication approaches him (Frei Caneca) to the common people'. Online at <http://www.ihuonline.unisinos.br/index.php?option=com_content&view=article&id=2852&secao=310> [accessed 9 May 2014]. Confounding the ecclesiastical degradation with excommunication compromises the interpretation of the poem, since one is a vindictive punishment and the other is the exclusion from a community of faith.

The basic theological key to interpreting these words, and what I would like to explore here in parallel to the words of Frei Caneca in *Auto do frade*, is well summarized in a text from 1964, by John Wilkinson, who divides them into three groups: three words of Intercession, two words of Suffering and two words of Victory,[15] explained in the following terms:

> In the first three words we see Jesus' concern for others. [...] Then the focus changes and the scene is centred on Himself as He undergoes the suffering to which He had surrendered Himself for the salvation of mankind. Thus we find that the last four words are concerned with Himself and His own experiences, and they are all uttered towards the end of His time on the Cross.[16]

I would like to explore whether it is possible to read the words of Frei Caneca within this same hermeneutic framework. I do not intend to compare the words literally, for the obvious reason that what is in the gospels are just short sentences of Christ, many of them being quotations from the Old Testament, perhaps prayers, while in João Cabral's poems the friar is more eloquent. My interest is to understand whether this structure of intercession, suffering and victory can be deduced from *Auto do frade*.

The first speech by the friar in the poem occurs in the second scene, at the jail door, when he is removed to start on his Way of the Cross:

> — Acordo fora de mim
> como há tempos não fazia.
>
> [...]
> Acordar é reacordar-se
> ao que em nosso redor gira
> mesmo quando alguém acorda
> para um fiapo de vida,
> como o que tanto aparato
> que me cerca me anuncia:
> esse bosque de espingardas
> mudas, mas logo assassinas.
> [...]
> Essas coisas me situam
> e também me dão saída;
> ao vê-las me vejo nelas,
> me completam, convividas.
> Não é o inerte acordar
> na cela negra e vazia:
> lá não podia dizer
> quando velava ou dormia.[17]

---

[15] John Wilkinson, 'The Seven Words from the Cross', *Scottish Journal of Theology*, 17.1 (March 1964), 69–82 (p. 69).
[16] Id. pp. 69–70.
[17] Cabral, *A Escola das Facas e Auto do Frade*, p. 114. Hereafter page numbers will be given in the text.

[I wake outside of myself | as I had not done in ages. | [...] To wake up is to re-awake | to what is around us | even when we awake | to a simple thread of life | like what surrounds me | is announcing: | this wood of guns | dumb, but soon-to-be murderers. [...] These things help situate me | and give me a way out; | I see myself in them, | they complete me, live with me. | It is not a mere awakening | in a dark and empty cell: | there I could not tell | whether I was awake or sleeping.]

This is not exactly the words of Christ: 'Father, forgive them for they know not what they do.' However, the poetic image is also geared towards an outer universe, outside of jail, out of yourself. What is curious is that Frei Caneca is already prophetic in predicting that he will be shot and not hanged, as sentenced in his conviction, and it is also noteworthy how, in a way, the friar does not personify those who will actually perform the action. His words are somehow interceding, because they remind him that what he sees gives him life, albeit briefly. He does not accuse and does not blaspheme. In terms of a Carmelite, he accepts the passion with perseverance and prophetically. The awareness and acceptance of sacrifice open his eyes.

In addition, it reminds us of another key motto for Carmelite mystique, that of the dark night of the soul, present in this mystical poetry of two other bastions of the Carmel, St John of the Cross and St Teresa of Avila. In both poems, a dark night precedes the last contemplation of God. It is interesting to see that João Cabral offers us an almost mystical Frei Caneca in his first words in the poem.

The Friar's second speech, on his way from jail to the Church of the Rosary, is again geared towards the outside, rather than to himself. It starts out by refusing his nickname as a saint: '— Se é procissão que me fazem | mudou muito a liturgia: | não vejo andor para o santo | nem há nenhum santo à vista' [— Whether it's procession that they make me | liturgy is much changed: | I do not see a platform for the saint, | nor is there a saint in sight] (p. 124). The friar continues describing his own funeral procession, with no tragedies or laments, and demonstrates his familiarity with the people who are present at his Via Dolorosa:

> Dessa gente sei dizer
> quem Manuel e quem Maria,
> quem boticário ou caixeiro,
> e sua mesma freguesia.
> Cada casa dessas ruas
> é também amiga íntima,
> posso dizer a cor que era;
> que no ano passado tinha. (p. 125)

[Of these people I can say | who is Manuel and who is Maria, | who is a herbalist or a salesman, | and where they come from. | In these streets, each house, | is also a close friend, | I can tell you what colour it once was; | last year.]

Caneca is not concerned with himself, or with death awaiting him. He refers to himself as dead, in anticipation of the passion. His eyes, however, remain focused outwards. He echoes Christ's 'Today shalt thou be with me in paradise' (Luke 23. 42). The Joes and Maries, herbalists and salesmen, are those who shared their life with Frei Caneca and for whom the Carmelite dedicates his existence and passion. They will also share his paradise with him.

Interestingly, this second word by the friar is motivated by the 'Gente nas calçadas' [People on the streets] themselves who would annoy him with their silence along the way by asking: '— por que será que ele não fala, | nem diz nada sua boca muda?' [why does he not speak | and his silent mouth say nothing?] (p. 124).

This silence leads to Frei Caneca's third word. It is the only time the friar engages in a short exchange in the poem, responding to the Officer who admonishes him for talking. The Officer asks him: '— de que fala Reverendíssimo | como se num sermão de missa?' [what are you talking about Reverend | as in sermon?] (p. 127). The friar's answer shows him as an intercessor: '— de toda essa luz do Recife. | Louvava-a nesta despedida' [of all the light of Recife. | I was praising it in my farewell] (p. 127). The Officer does not seem to be convinced and insists: '— ouvi-o falar em voz alta, | como se celebrasse missa. | Vi que a gente pelas calçadas | como num sermão, calada, ouvia' [I heard him speaking out loud, | as if celebrating mass. | I saw people on the streets, | listening, quietly, as though to a sermon] (p. 127). And after Frei Caneca's contemplative response, he declares peremptorily: '— Um condenado não pode falar. | Condenado à morte, perde a língua' [A condemned man cannot speak. | Sentenced to death, he loses his tongue] (p. 127). The friar's conclusion takes us back to the value and meaning of silence as a promoter of justice, for a Carmelite: '— Passarei a falar em silêncio. | Assim está salva a Disciplina' [I will speak in silence. | Thus discipline will be safeguarded] (p. 127).

Following the proposed hermeneutic path and comparing Frei Caneca's words in the poem with Christ's last words, the words of intercession have ended, those which demonstrate 'concern for others'. Frei Caneca's next speech, still on his way from jail to the Church of the Rosary, follows the theology of the seven words, thus inaugurating the 'words of suffering'.

Awareness of the approaching passion becomes reality and more visible. The perception of the short time he has left, enough time just for this walk, makes him turn to what he will suffer: 'Eu sei que no fim de tudo | um poço cego me fita' [I know that at the end | a dark well will be staring at me] (p. 130).

Frei Caneca's fifth word is uttered still on this same path from jail to the Church of the Rosary, and, again, João Cabral puts regret and suffering in the Friar's mouth. In a soliloquy in which he compares his apostolate with a surveyor's work he regrets that the act of building a fair world is not as easy as that of drawing it on paper:

> sei que traçar no papel
> é mais fácil que na vida.
> Sei que o mundo jamais é
> a página pura e passiva. (p. 133)

[I know that tracing on paper | is easier than in real life. | I know that the world is never | a pure and passive page.]

In this speech João Cabral reveals another interesting aspect of the life of Frei Caneca. The speech of the Carmelite is full of Masonic metaphors, an institution the friar, like many other religious people in Brazil, belonged to. The relationship between geometry and the world is sought and political action is seen as undergoing a divine architecture. However, the friar regrets not having achieved the construction of this idealized world.

The following scene is the aforementioned stripping of the holy orders by the ecclesiastical degradation ritual, so that the friar could be given over to secular justice and have his sentence performed. The poem is descriptive and explanatory, reproducing the Latin prayers and items pertaining to this ritual. Frei Caneca is completely silent.

It is on his way from the Church of the Rosary, where he was stripped of his orders, to Praça do Forte, where he will be executed, that the Carmelite speaks again. What first strikes us is that he re-states his status as a Carmelite: 'Eis as pedras do Recife | que o professo carmelita, | embora frade calçado, | sente na sola despida' [Here are the stones of Recife | whom I declare as a Carmelite, | although not barefoot, | I feel them as such] (p. 148). And then, even closer to death, he proves to be victorious over this same death. Like a clairvoyant, he states: 'Parece que melhor vejo, | que levo lentes na vista; | se antes tudo isso milvi; | as coisas estão mais nítidas' [It seems I see better, | as though through lenses; | if before I saw things repeatedly; | things are even clearer now] (p. 149). And he finishes his sixth monologue with a sense of triumphant hope and persistence: 'quem sabe um dia virá | uma civil geometria?' [who knows | one day we might see a civil geometry?] (p. 149).

In the friar's last speech, João Cabral conjures up a series of mystical images, completing the passion of Frei Caneca and giving it a sense beyond history. Even after being deprived of the holy robe, Caneca transforms his shroud into a sacrificial robe, making it new. He may no longer be able to celebrate the Mass, but offers himself in sacrifice, as the Christ.

Images that are dear to the negative theology of St John of the Cross, mixed with timeless and atopic ramblings by the friar, grant him a communion with eternity. A typical metaphor of the mystical apophatic discourse is present: the colour white. Colour and colourlessness at the same time, presence and absence:

> Será que a morte é de branco,
> onde coisa não habita,
> ou, se habita, dá na soma
> uma brancura negativa? (p. 152)

[Might death be white, | where nothing exists, | or if it does, it is a sum | of negative whiteness?]

The soliloquy continues with the acceptance of death by the friar — not desperately or dramatically, but triumphantly. Passion will be completed and a sense of salvation is understood in it. As in the last words of Christ on the cross, 'Father, into thy hands I commend my spirit', Caneca also commends his spirit, not without acknowledging the fear that death causes him, but embracing, with a Carmelite devotion, the imitation of the Passion of the Christ: 'Se essa mortalha branca | é bilhete que habilita | a essa morte, eu, que a receio, | entro nela com alegria. | Temo a morte, embora saiba | que é uma conta devida' [If this white shroud | is a ticket to | this death, I, who fear it, | enter it with joy. | I fear death, although I know | that it is a debt that must be paid] (pp. 152–53)

Thus, Frei Caneca's seven monologues in João Cabral's poem travel through the same exegetical perspective as the words of Christ on the cross, according to Catholic tradition. Moreover, we can see in the words and silences of Frei Caneca a clear perception of Carmelite spirituality as it relates to perseverance in the imitation of Christ, even if it leads to passion.

In this final speech by Frei Caneca, *Auto do frade* suggests a nod to *Morte e vida severina*, thereby suggesting some kind of closure in relation to the *autos*. Through the words of Frei Caneca, the young Severino born in the Christmas *auto* delivers his spirit at the end of this Way of the Cross of the Passion *auto*.

> Devemos todos a Deus
> o preço de nossa vida
> e a pagamos com a morte
> (o poeta inglês já dizia).
> Nesta contabilidade
> morte e vida se equilibram,
> e, embora no livro caixa,
> e também nas estatísticas,
> apareça favorável,
> e sempre, o saldo da vida,
> no dia do fim do mundo
> serão iguais as partidas. (p. 153)

[We all owe God | the price of our life | and we pay it with death | (as the English poet already said). | In these accounts | death and life are equal, | and although in the log book, | and also in statistics, | what appears greater | is always life, | on the day of the end of the world | the two will be the same.]

Níobe Abreu Peixoto exemplarily summarizes this relationship between *Auto do frade* and *Morte e vida severina*, realizing how we can read both poems in a hermeneutical horizon of the Salvation history:

> Frei Caneca vem se juntar a Severino, que também age em busca de uma vida melhor. No entanto, o alcance das duas caminhadas não é o mesmo. A diferença está na ideologia do carmelita. A possibilidade de escolha,

a consciência de justição social e do peso da ação coletiva têm correspondência na voz plural do Auto do frade. [...] Utopia e racionalidade, nos mesmos versos.[18]

[Frei Caneca joins Severino, who also is moved by the search for a better life. However, the ranges of the two paths are not the same. The difference is the ideology of the Carmelite. The possibility of choice, the awareness of social justice and the weight of collective action find correspondence in the plural voice of *Auto do frade* [...] Utopia and rationality, in the same lines.]

Caneca does not die for the salvation of mankind, as Christ does, but for his ideals and utopias. He is aware that his political choices led him to the gallows, but also that these same choices were responsible for the refusal of all possible hangmen to kill him, forcing the sentence to be changed from hanging to shooting; another victory over death, which instead of degrading becomes honourable. Frei Caneca, the historical character, also wrote verses. In one of his last poems, written when he was already in prison, the friar defends passion and accepts it as inevitable in the quest for a utopian society:

> Para defender a pátria
> Menino homem se faz,
> Em dando a vida por ela;
> Morrendo, não peno mais.
>
> [...]
>
> Inda que eu queira, não posso
> Existir entre os mortais.
> A morte serve de alívio;
> Morrendo, não peno mais.
>
> Oh! morte, por que não vens
> Findar meus dias fatais?
> Se vivo, vivo penando;
> Morrendo, não peno mais.[19]

[To defend the homeland | Boy becomes man, | In giving my life for her; | Dying, no more I will grieve. | [...] | Even wishing, I cannot | Exist among mortals. | Death serves as a relief; | Dying, no more I will grieve. | Oh! death, why do not you come | to end my fatal days? | If alive, I live grieving; | Dying, no more I will grieve. ]

In this comparative analysis between the passion of Frei Caneca according to João Cabral de Melo Neto and the Passion of the Christ, the last scene in the *auto* must occupy a special place. Indeed it is the only one in prose, just a description of how Frei Caneca's body, after being shot, is deposited by anonymous people at the door to the Basilica of Mount Carmel and then collected by the friars who

---

[18] Níobe Abreu Peixoto, *João Cabral e o poema dramático: Auto do Frade (poema para vozes)* (São Paulo: Anablume, FAPESP, 2001), p. 55.
[19] Frei Caneca, *Para Defender a Pátria*, online at <http://www.dominiopublico.br> [accessed 9 May 2014].

take it into the Church, in a clear illusion to the burial of Christ. Historically, it is not known what became of Frei Caneca's body; the exact location of his grave is not known. He was presumably buried in the convent, according to tradition, but this is not known for sure. In other words, his body is not in the tomb, like that of the risen Christ.

Thus, it is important to return to the beginning of the poem and to the dialogue between the jailer and the provincial about sleep and death. At the end of the poem, the relationship between the Passion of the Christ and that of Frei Caneca complement each other in understanding the meaning of death as simply a sleep, a concept referred to by Christ in the Gospels, when he resurrects a girl and says she was only sleeping (Mark 5. 39), and also when he resurrects Lazarus, once again stating that he was only sleeping (John 11. 11). The greater sense of the Passion of the Christ, and especially what lies behind the seven words of Christ on the cross is that, again with Wilkinson, 'Death is but a sleep, and to die is but to fall asleep.'[20]

## Until Time is Completed, or by Way of Conclusion

In this article I have sought to read *Auto do frade* by looking at the close parallels it draws with the Passion of the Christ. This occurs especially when the friar speaks in the *Auto*, seven times, and I have compared these utterances with the seven words of Christ on the cross. To understand whether a parallel would be possible and how we could read this *auto* as an *auto* of passion, I presented the exegetical framework into which the words of Christ on the cross fall, within the theological concept of the plan of salvation, and also seek the value and space given to the passion within the spirituality and mysticism of the Carmelite order, to which Frei Caneca belonged. In this case, we can infer how certain values are associated with the construction of this Carmelite spirituality and mysticism, such as perseverance, prophetism and silence, and how these can be read in João Cabral's poem. This also demonstrates how *Auto do frade* completes a cycle in conjunction with *Morte e vida severina*, another dramatic poem with a religious theme, this time the birth of a child parallel to the birth of Christ.

However, we can understand João Cabral not as being an orthodox religious apologetic poet, but as a poet who reads the history of salvation in the history of his own people and expresses it as a poetic theology of hope and freedom. *Auto do frade* is a poem which, because it is religious, speaks politically, and which, paradoxically, by being political, is also religious. Despite being a poet who peremptorily declared he did not believe in any religion and being quite far from a religious confession, João Cabral could see in religiosity and North-Eastern traditions a motto for a prophetic voice, which is freed from a poetry

---

[20] Wilkinson, 'The Seven Words from the Cross', p. 82.

that becomes mystical, even if this is not its intent. In *Auto do frade*, one of João Cabral's later works, the poem takes on a prophetic tone and articulates a voice which is persevering, which does not deny the passion and that, after the silence of the poet, follows on eloquently denouncing and announcing.

# The Extreme and Geometry: Notes on João Cabral de Melo Neto's collection on Bullfighting and his Poetic Imagery

FLORA SÜSSEKIND

*Centro de Letras e Artes (UNIRIO) and
Fundação Casa de Rui Barbosa (Rio de Janeiro)*

This article offers a brief study of João Cabral de Melo Neto's process of image construction and — without disregarding the analyses provided in this respect by critics such as Antonio Cândido, Luiz Costa Lima, Haroldo de Campos, Othon Moacyr Garcia and João Alexandre Barbosa — it takes as its starting point the discovery of a small collection of materials on bullfighting which the poet started to put together during the period in which he lived in Barcelona in the late 1940s, and which surprisingly would remain intact throughout the poet's many travels and periods spent living abroad. Stored in a cardboard folder, this collection remained forgotten on the top of a wardrobe at his home in Rio de Janeiro right up to his death, in 1999.

Strictly speaking, it comes as no news that João Cabral de Melo Neto had a deep interest in Spanish culture. This would grow, of course, thanks to the periods he spent in Barcelona and Seville and it would remain an important reference in his writing career, not only in themes, but in rhythms, structure, make-up and development of his poetic work. Indeed, what this find seems to demonstrate relates not only to Cabral's relationship with Spain, something he frequently referred to, but equally to a dialogue (so far generally overlooked) between the poet and dissident wings within the surrealist movement (in particular the group around the journal *Documents*, later congregating around André Breton and the publication *Minotaure*) and a figural method which, like the art of bullfighting, would have as its basic formulations the definition of places of contact, the calculated use of processes of (self-)development and concentric circles, the tension between an aesthetic of the bodily gesture and the language of geometry, between lucidity and intensity, between displacement and approximation, the production of distances and situations of defiance and confrontation.

This article will not, therefore, simply reiterate a repertoire of images and themes which are known to feature in Cabral's work, by revisiting them through the items found in the collection, but it will consider them from a different perspective. Thus, it will consider such a repertoire as visible manifestation of a

FIG. 1. Los Toreros Trágicos [The Tragic Bullfighters].
Back cover of The Kon Leche Crônica Tauromáquica Ano VII, num 241, 22 April 1918

structural dialogue between poetics. We are indeed dealing with poetics, given that what I will discuss here is based on a complex play with certain technical rules, with norms, with the dissolutions and displacements which characterize certain practices of both bullfighting and literary composition. These also point to an affinity (usually absolutely denied by Cabral) with certain surrealist imagery — having as its point of reference, in the case of series on bullfighters and bulls, mainly the work of Michel Leiris, Georges Bataille and André Masson. It also points to dialogues with other Cabral contemporaries, of quite diverse artistic inclinations — from Gertrude Stein to Orson Welles, from Pablo Picasso to Abel Gance, from Joan Mirò to Ernest Hemingway. All of these, at some point and to different degrees, investigated the relationship between the play between violence and precision, balance and instability, and the notion of beauty which defined bullfighting and how it was reflected upon aesthetically in other artistic media.

Another aspect which the small collection suggests is the strong link between Cabral's series of poems on bullfighters and bullfighting and his careful study of the photographic material, the available bibliography and newspaper columns in the Spanish press dedicated to the art of bullfighting. Indeed, Cabral seems to have engaged consciously with what the reports from bullfighting scenes and episodes suggested with regard to the style of different bullfighters and different bull species. In fact, his poems would often include epithets and stories directly reproduced from newspaper accounts about this bullfighter or the other. In the case of Manolete, especially, Cabral seems to have examined a large number of photographs of the bullfighter's postures and gestures in different bullfights with particular attention.

Yet, if this selection of cuttings and images points to, on the one hand, a deliberately documentary approach in relation to the poetic representation of bullfighting, on the other, one can at the same time detect a more speculative tendency, involving reflections on a possible theory of bullfighting itself, of bullfighting as a 'mindgame'. This is evidenced by Cabral's decision to keep the cutting of an article by José María Gutiérrez Ballesteros and the image of the manuscript by Amós Salvador on bullfighting and geometry.[1] Cabral's careful preservation of such materials, alongside his study of the movements and strategies employed by various bullfighters, of the differences between classic and modern bullfighting, which he scrutinized through the photos to hand, as well as the echoes we detect in his writing of essays on bullfighting such as those by Michel Leiris and José Bergamin, appear to have been crucial in bringing about a change in the process of image construction in Cabral's poetry which was already apparent in a poem such as *O cão sem plumas*, for

---

[1] Amós Salvador Rodrigáñez (1845-1922) was a Spanish politician, writer and engineer, author of various studies among which 'Sobre la perspectiva lineal para uso de la pintura'. His 'Teoria del toreo', written between 1 and 15 May 1908, was initially published in fragments in magazines and eventually published by the Unión de Bibliófilos Taurinos in 1962.

example. This study is, therefore, not so much about the collection itself, but above all about its relevance for the change that occurred in Cabral's poetic practice, and its relation to the features that would come to define Cabral's figural constructions.

## The Collection

I believe it is, however, first necessary to return to the collection, given that it is the link between what we can verify in some poems as a closer relationship between the poet and certain surrealist tendencies, between writing and a registration of the real, and aspects related to the theory of bullfighting and a significant shift in his figural method. In this respect, it is important to give a description, albeit a brief one here, of the items that make up the collection. I will, therefore, begin by giving some context of how, almost by accident, I came to have access to material the importance of which (beyond its purely documentary value) resides in the signalling of structural changes in Cabral's poetry, and therefore of fundamental changes in his poetics.

Two years after Cabral's death, at a time when his heirs were negotiating rights over the flat where he had lived in Praia do Flamengo, in Rio de Janeiro, part of his private library was put up for sale at bookshops in Rio and São Paulo. Among the material set aside, there appeared at Livraria Berinjela, in Rio de Janeiro, a folder which failed to attract any buyers and which contained a series of cuttings, photos, newspapers and magazines, a large part of them dating back to the period between 1947 and 1950, during which time the poet had been Brazilian vice-consul in Barcelona.

Thanks to Daniel Chomsky, one of the owners of the second-hand bookshop on Rua Marques do Herval, in Rio's city centre, the folder would end up in my possession at a time when I was working on the edition of the correspondence between Cabral and fellow Brazilian poets Manuel Bandeira (1886–1968) and Carlos Drummond de Andrade (1902–1987) at the Research Centre of the Fundação Casa de Rui Barbosa. Some of the old images, reproductions of magazines and Spanish newspaper cuttings, would actually be included as illustrations in the volume published in 2001 by Editora Nova Fronteira, to accompany the edition of letters, together with other images and copies of manuscripts.

The ensemble of cuttings, photos and periodicals included in this unexpected collection belonging to Cabral is not, as I have mentioned, very substantial. It is practically all in fact dedicated to bullfighting, to some bullfighters, to the description of bullrings and the 'ganaderías' [cattle breeders] in Spain, with the exception of an issue of Manchete magazine which focused on the construction and inauguration of the new Brazilian capital, Brasília, curiously filed away among the bullfighting archive. This might have been due to some desire to file materials according to a chronological order, since the bullfighting cuttings cover a period from 1910 to the late 1950s. In this sense, the construction of the new Brazilian capital, from 1956 to 1960, with the first plans drafted in 1954, would fit into the chronological rationale of the collection's organization. But not only chronological, however, because the constructive rigour of the 'plano piloto' [city plan] designed by engineer Lúcio Costa and of the architectural designs by Oscar Niemeyer engaged with the relationship between the concept of the city and geometry. In the light of this, it is possible to infer that the dialogue they established on an architectural level could have suggested to the poet-collector an association with the hypothesis elaborated by Amós Salvador about the possibility of thinking about bullfighting in geometrical terms, though there are no annotations in the collection that might confirm this connection.

The archive is made up of a total of forty-five items — one of which is a collection of fifteen photos signed by Gonsanhi (with the indication of an address — 'Mallorca, 206' — and telephone number — '79877' — in Barcelona), all of them of the bullfight in Linares in which the famous bullfighter Manolete (1917–1947) was killed. Aside from this, there is a series of copies of posters of Manolete's last bullfight, dated 28 August 1947, signed by Pedrosan and entitled 'Asi toreaba... Asi murió' [This is how he fought... This is how he died]. And there are several periodicals referring to this death, such as the special issue 'Cogida y Muerte de Manolete' from *Semanario Gráfico* (of 30 August 1947), a series of photos of the Plaza de Toros of Linares taken by Francisco Cano, the photojournalist responsible for the image that captured the exact moment when the bullfighter, having launched the final thrust against the bull Islero, would himself be fatally gored, at the age of thirty, on 29 August 1947. The photographer would describe the moment as the one when Manuel Rodriguez Sánchez, known as Manolete, 'matou morrendo ou morreu matando' [killed while dying or died while killing].

The bullfighter died soon after Cabral's move to Barcelona, in April that same year, and the poet would recall how he had seen Manolete fight twice, leaving no doubt in letters and interviews as to the impact that the spectacle had on him. Not only because of the visual impact of Manolete's distinctive mode of fighting, but also because of the shock at the news of the matador's premature death and the shockwaves it sent throughout Spain and on the international news, Manolete having previously announced his intention to retire from bullfighting on 19 October that year, as we read in an interview published in the magazine *Aqui está*, dated 7 August 1947. Thus, it is not surprising to discover that the majority of the newspaper cuttings and entire issues of magazines on bullfighting included in the collection relate to the career, death and burial of Manolete.

Just to mention some of the items belonging to Cabral's small collection, we find, for example, a cutting from *La prensa*, of 29 August, featuring the title 'Manolete morto por um touro em Linhares' [Manolete killed by a bull in Linares]. This is one of several similar articles selected by the poet, such as the cover 'Nasceu o dia e morreu o toureiro' [The day breaks and the matador dies], from the Madrid newspaper *Diario de la noche*, of 30 August 1947, and the article 'El llanto de la ciudad' [The tears of the city], in *La vanguardia española*. Then there are the photos which accompany publications on Manolete's death, such as those showing the dying or dead matador, or earlier images which give the publication a melancholic feel, such as the one taken from the 30 August edition of *Hola*, in which Manolete is seen beside his mother and niece. There are other images of him illustrating the pages of publications such as the *Diario de Barcelona* and *La vanguardia española*, of 31 August of that same year, with coverage of his funeral. These articles would be followed by others published in these same newspapers and recording the impact of Manolete's death ouside of Spain.

Indeed, the cuttings relating to Manolete are numerous, some published prior to his death in Linares, but a clear majority linked directly to his death. In fact, the matador's death seems to be the reason behind Cabral's methodical organization of the collection, with photos of Manolete smoking, Manolete among writers, a silent Manolete, Manolete and his recent triumphs in Mexico, and so on. And alongside a rich photographic collection, which allows a careful observation of his movements, his behaviour and his mode of bullfighting, there are also items about the myths surrounding the matador, which became *topoi* around this figure, and analyses which single him out within the modern bullfighting tradition.

From the point of view of the creation of myths within the bullring, there is a section from a September 1947 issue of *Los toros* which includes texts which are exemplary, given that all pay posthumous homage to the matador. Among these is the long poem by Rafael Duyos, entitled 'Manolete, su muerte, su arcangel y su toro' [Manolete, his death, his archangel, and his bull]. Among the special publications, such as the edition of *Fotos-Marca* on the 'Vida, triunfo y muerte de Manolete' [Life, triumph and death of Manolete], Cabral would include not just anecdotes about his life, posthumous eulogies or romanticized versions of his biography, but many items related to the analysis of his bullfighting style. We find this in an issue of the magazine *Dígame*, of 9 September 1947, entitled 'Presencia y ausencia de Manolete' [Presence and absence of Manolete], which includes miscellanea that go from a self-caricature to a selection of stories on bullfighting which attempted to go beyond the merely anecdotal and described details and episodes from the Miura ranch, where the bull Islero had been bred and referring to bullfighting experts on Manolete, among them Ricardo Garcia (pseudonym 'K-Hito'), who had recently completed a book on the matador.

Incidentally, it would be K-Hito who would play the key role in sealing Manolete's reputation as a bullfighter in Madrid. In his column on the fight which took place on 12 October 1939, for instance, he had already identified the defining features of Manolete's practice, which he referred to as a 'more subtle baroque', noting in it a *'temple* [steadiness], a slowness, a gentleness', alongside 'perfect moves with the red cape, refined, correct', of huge impact, which led the bull 'at a slow pace', in 'smooth movements, of unique beauty'. Reading these remarks by K-Hito, it is hard not to be reminded of Cabral's definition of the rhythm of his poetry, as when he referred to poems 'com passo de prosa' [with the step of prose],[2] or when he tried to explain to his fellow poet Manuel Bandeira how Manolete was an almost speculative bullfighter. In particular, in a letter dated 4 September 1947, he would comment on the death of the bullfighter, drawing attention above all to the slowness of his movements, the gestures which reminded him of those of a sower and comparing him in his precision to a 'bullfighting Paul Valéry'.[3]

Yet, it is not just the columnist K-Hito who seems to be echoed in some of Cabral's comments on the art of bullfighting. The photos by Francisco Cano of the bullfight at Linares, showing the bodies of Manolete and of Islero almost touching, seem to be recreated, for example, through the use of the verb 'roçar' [to brush/rub against] in the poem 'Alguns toureiros' (of the collection *Paisagens com figuras*, 1956), while emphasis is placed on the daring character of the fight underlined in 'Lembrando Manolete' (*Agrestes*, 1985). Indeed, Cabral's mini-collection points to some unexpected dialogues related to the development of some of his poetry's stylistic features and bullfighting analogies. It also draws our attention to the degree to which some of these dialogues — which I will consider in the section that follows — can be seen to have contributed to some significant aesthetic changes.

## Theories on Bullfighting

Let us return, however, to the photos by Francisco Cano and their caption in the special issue of *Fotos-Marca*, and to the reference to the final thrust against Islero: 'In this photo, we see perfectly the encounter between a bull and the bullfighter, Manolete digging the sword into Islero and the bull plunging his horn into Manolete's young body.' And let us go back once more to the poem 'Alguns toureiros', in order to consider the caption quoted above and lines taken from the poem, in which Cabral attempted to define Manolete as 'o que melhor calculava | o fluido aceiro da vida | o que com mais precisão | roçava a morte em sua fímbria' [the one who best calculated | the fluid clearing of life | the one who with greatest precision | brushed death with his hem].[4]

The poem appears almost deliberately to quote the iconography and myth-ology of proximity which were rightly associated with the bullfighter. We

---

[2] See Flora Süssekind, 'Com passo de prosa: voz, figura e movimento na poesia de João Cabral de Melo Neto', *Revista USP*, 16 (1992–93), 93–102.
[3] See Flora Süssekind (ed.), *Correspondência de Cabral com Bandeira e Drummond* (Rio de Janeiro: Nova Fronteira; Fundação Casa de Rui Barbosa, 2001), p. 34.
[4] In João Cabral de Melo Neto, *Obra completa* (Rio de Janeiro: Nova Aguilar, 1994), p. 158. All quotations of Cabral's poetry are taken from this edition unless otherwise stated.

Fig. 2. Images of Manolete at the Plaza de Toros in Madrid, 1944.

need only recall the content of some of the pages from the issue of *Dígame* devoted to paying homage to Manolete and dedicated to explaining 'how he would bullfight', highlighting the 'stoicism with which he would endure, at unbelievable close range, the attacks from the animals'. Indeed, if 'in the days of Belmonte' it seemed impossible to 'get closer to the bulls', after Manolete it was a case of 'the bulls having to move away from the range of the bullfighter'. Yet, in the references made to Manolete in Cabral's poem quoted above there is not only an emphasis on the need for proximity but also of measured response and precision. The poem refers to the bullfighter with whom Cabral appeared to have felt greater affinity as one who 'à tragédia deu número, | à vertigem, geometria, | decimais à emoção | e ao susto, peso e medida' [gave a number to tragedy, | geometry to vertigo, | decimals to emotion | and a weight and measure to fear] (p. 158).

If the geometry identified by the poet in Manolete's approach brings it closer to Cabral's own poetics of construction, which he had explored since the publication of his collection *O engenheiro* (1946),[5] it also reminds us of some of the most significant theories on bullfighting being debated during the first half of the twentieth century and which, like Amós Salvador's theory, of 1908, seemed to suggest that 'bullfighting is all a question of geometry'.

As for the connection between Cabral and Manolete, it is revisited in the closing lines of 'Alguns toureiros', where Cabral in turn alludes to his earlier composition 'Antiode' (1947) by suggesting for both poetry and bullfighting a 'mão certa, pouca e extrema: | sem perfumar sua flor, | sem poetizar seu poema' [a precise, small and extreme hand: | without perfuming its flower, | without poeticizing its poem] (p. 158). This connection would reverberate in certain recurring poetic analogies, such as that between the act of writing and confrontation, between river and bull, since the latter has 'o mesmo atropelar | cego da água' [the same blind | stampede of water], 'os mesmos redemoinhos | da cheia' [the same whirlpools | of the flood], as we read in 'El toro de Lidia', of *Museu de tudo* (1975). The connection is also made in the analogies of sea and bull, such as in the description of the sea and the rivers of Recife as 'touros de índole distinta' [bulls of different disposition] (p. 386) of the poem 'As águas do Recife', also of *Museu de tudo*, or between words and bulls, since 'onde foi palavra | (potros ou touros | contidos) resta a severa | forma do vazio' [where there was the word | (colts or bulls | restrained) there remains the severe | form of emptiness] (p. 97), in 'Psicologia da composição', of 1947.

Connections and analogies such as these are not, however, the only features to reveal the significance of bullfighting imagery in Cabral's poetic trajectory. Indeed, it is a trait that emerges constantly throughout his work, such as in the image of the 'viver no aceiro da morte' [life in the clearing of death] (p. 679) of the Sevillians ('A imaginação perigosa', *Andando Sevilha* (1992)). It also

---

[5] See in this respect Haroldo de Campos's study, 'O geometra engajado', in *Metalinguagem* (São Paulo: Cultrix, 1978), pp. 67–78.

Fig. 3. Image of Manolete in Valencia, 1944

appears in the numerous anecdotes about flamenco dancers and bullfighters that found their way into Cabral's poems (see the poems referring to the suicide of Juan Belmonte, or the death of José Gallito),[6] as well as in the many recurring references to Manolete and his precise economy of movements. The association of bullfighting with geometry would also feature prominently in Cabral's poetry — through allusions to the decimals, measures, weight, and the vertigo associated with Manolete's particular method of fighting, as well as the wisdom of Gallito, another acclaimed bullfighter whose skill Cabral associates with geometry.

If bullfighting perceived as a form of geometry would define its treatment within Cabral's work, such a perspective is also one of the key approaches we can identify in the newspaper articles and studies on bullfighting and one which would define efforts over the course of the first half of the twentieth century to elevate bullfighting as art, as a 'major theme' and accompanying the process of modernization of bullfighting practices which would have in Joselito, Belmonte and Manolete its key figures. Among the different sources defending an approach to bullfighting as a form of geometry is one actually included in Cabral's small collection on bullfighting, namely in the issue of *Dígame* of 19 March 1948, in which José María Gutiérrez Ballesteros would attempt to synthesize Amós Salvador's theories. As critic José Guilherme Merquior suggested in his book *A astúcia da mímese*,[7] a similar approach would be

---

[6] See 'Juan Belmonte' (*Andando Sevilha*, 1992) and 'A morte de "Gallito"' (*Crime na Calle Relator*, 1987).
[7] José Guilherme Merquior, 'Nuvem civil sonhada — ensaio sobre a poética de João Cabral de Melo

attempted by Cabral, he argued, in an 'anthology of images' from his previous books in 'Alguns toureiros', in the form of a 'poetic equivalent' of bullfighting studies such as those elaborated by Michel Leiris and possibly, among others, also by José Bergamin.

As regards the theory on bullfighting by Amós Salvador Rodrigáñez, written between 1 and 15 May 1908 and only published in book form in 1962, Cabral would keep in his collection of cuttings and journals on bullfighting a copy of the 19 March 1948 issue of *Dígame*, in which José María Gutiérrez Ballesteros would summarize the relationship between bullfighting and geometry. The geometrical dimension of bullfighting would emerge both in specific features linked to the matador's performance, for example, (such as the need for the sword to hit the bull at an angle of 45 degrees along the line that follows its spinal cord thus increasing its potential to kill), and in more general aspects, such as the general layout of the ring in relation to the movement and positions of the bull during the fight.

On the space where the fighting takes place, Amós Salvador Rodrigáñez states that when 'the bull comes out the bullring (i.e. the larger circle) belongs entirely to it.' Given that the ring is made up of concentric circles, the bull gradually loses space as the matador takes over, up to the point of the 'supreme fate', when the centre of these circles is marked by the spot where the back of the animal and the sword make contact. In relation to the movements by the bull and its direction, Amós Salvador Rodrigáñez defines them in terms of curves and countercurves, deploying terms normally used when describing the process of drawing. He speaks of each direction taken as drawing an involute curve and each position of the head of the animal as giving rise, by opposite effect, to an evolute, in turn linked to those outlined by the movements of the matador.

If the article by Ballesteros divulged to a wider public the relationship between bullfighting and geometry developed by Amós Salvador Rodrigáñez in his then still unpublished theory, it does not follow that he provided the link between Cabral's bullfighting imagery and the association he made with features of intensity and rigour, but it is significant that Cabral should decide to keep precisely the cutting of Ballesteros's piece. It is also relevant to remember that if his collection included various texts on Manolete, reports on bullfighting, on 'Juan Belmonte, El genio taurómaco de la época moderna' [Juan Belmonte, the bullfighting genius of the modern period], it had the summary of Amós Salvador's piece as one of its main items. And if this originally dated back to 1908, remaining relatively unknown up until the late 1940s, other studies on bullfighting (certainly known to Cabral) would also discuss the tension between violence and geometry as one of the structural elements of the practice and observation of bullfighting.

Such is the case of the writings by José Bergamin, in particular his 'Arte

Neto' in *A astúcia da mímese: ensaios sobre crítica* (Rio de Janeiro: José Olympio/Conselho Estadual de Cultura, 1972), pp. 69–172.

de birlibirloque' [art by magic], where he defined the fight as an 'admirable spectacle of passion and grace, of natural energy and conscious geometrical control',[8] in which 'the bull despises anything that isn't an exact and luminous confrontation' (p. 27) and the bullfighter 'must trick it with mathematical precision', with 'clear, fast and decisive' attention. In this essay, Bergamin deploys geometrical binaries to oppose curves and straight lines as he argues against Belmonte's manner of bullfighting (seen as slow, in straight tangential lines and exercises in approximation), which he viewed as something of a fraud, and viewing the practice in which curves, speed and distance from the bull are prevailing features, in the style adopted by the bullfighter Joselito, as a model of the vibrant qualities of bullfighting. Indeed, according to Bergamin, the curve 'defies the draughtsman, forcing him to express himself: in other words to think, to be a draughtsman, to adopt a style' (p. 32). Some years later, Bergamin would return to this opposition, rethinking his own dismissal of Juan Belmonte and concluding that it is impossible to think of the 'angelic' Joselito without the 'evil' Belmonte, given that 'if one (José) was Mozart, the other (Belmonte) was Beethoven', and he also underlined the creative qualities of the latter who 'with his short steps' had created his own 'stuttering manner of bullfighting'.

As far as Cabral's interest in Bergamin is concerned, it is perhaps important to remember that a few years ago a copy of the first edition of *Al volver*, by the Spanish writer, and featuring Cabral's signature and the reference 'Seville, 1962', was auctioned. Also noteworthy are their shared thoughts on 'silent music', the music which eludes melody, which at times does not sound, within Spanish culture. We might also recall the relevance of the *cante hondo*, of the driest style musical within flamenco, for Cabral's thoughts on diction and rhythm, and Bergamin's reflections on bullfighting's 'silent and lonely sound', seeing it as a spectacle which, he argues, 'has its own music, its silent music and music for the eyes'. It is true that points of contact between Cabral and Bergamin would become evident over the years, but it would have been difficult for Cabral, during his period in Spain in the 1940s, not to have come across Bergamin's study, published the previous decade.

Moreover, as his interest in bullfighting grew, it would have been difficult for him not to have read Michel Leiris's essay on literature as bullfighting, written in 1945 and 1946.[9] And it would be difficult not to consider the significance of this essay, as Merquior (1972) suggested, in the development of an aesthetic of the extreme and of precision in Cabral's work. Leiris's wish to 'escrever um livro que representasse um ato' [write a book that might represent an act] and which might equate 'àquilo que é para o toureiro o chifre acerado do touro' [to that which for the bullfighter is the sharp horn of the bull], able to confer 'reality' to art (Leiris, pp. 17–23), seems to echo considerably in the 'fazer no extremo, onde

---

[8] José Bergamin, *A arte de birlibirloque* (São Paulo: Hedra, 2012), p. 25.
[9] See Michel Leiris, 'De literatura como tauromaquia', in *A idade viril* (São Paulo: Cosac & Naify, 2003).

o risco começa' [making on the extreme, where risk begins] (p. 344), of Cabral's poem 'Coisas de cabeceira, Sevilha' (*A educação pela pedra*, 1966).

But if Leiris's thoughts seem to echo in certain formulations by Cabral, their dialogue would not be circumscribed to Leiris's essay on literature and bullfighting. An earlier 1938 study by the French writer entitled 'The Mirror of Bullfighting', and more specifically the image he developed of the 'figure of tangency' as a geometrical feature which distinguishes the art and the philosophy of bullfighting, seems central to understanding the change in Cabral's processes of figuration, particularly in poems from *O cão sem plumas* onwards.

### The Figure of (Almost) Tangency

If writings such as those by Amós Salvador (and their summary by Ballesteros), newspaper reports on bullfights, works such as those by Bergamin and Leiris, artists like André Masson, Miró and Picasso, are relevant to Cabral's poetic reflections on bullfighting (on the notions of risk and calculation) and to the importance it would acquire as an aesthetic paradigm in his work, and if the wealth of images and news cuttings on bullfighting, to which he had access during his first period living in Spain, already point to the significance of this thematic and image repertoire, there would be more to Cabral's relationship with bullfighting, however, something which would contribute decisively to a shift in his figural method.

Leiris's 'Mirror of Bullfighting' seems fundamental in this. Yet, before we consider him, let us recall some of the best studies on the use of imagery in Cabral's poetry. These include that of Luiz Costa Lima, who highlighted the 'explosões domadas' [tamed explosions] we find there, the 'contínua desmontagem (interna) da cadeia imagética' [constant (internal) breaking up of the chain of images].[10] We should also mention João Alexandre Barbosa's writings on the dominance of 'uma linguagem intensificadora e não apenas nomeante' [an intensifying language and not merely referential].[11] Also important to mention is the (sometimes overlooked) analysis by Othon Moacyr Garcia, in 'A página branca e o deserto', and its emphasis on Cabral's 'limitado repertório de idéias-matrizes' [limited repertoire of matrix-ideas], which work as 'núcleos de um sistema ondulatório e multifacetado de idéias' [nuclei of a shifting, multifaceted system of ideas], linked 'à primeira (à matriz) por alguma relação de afinidade' [to the first (matrix) by some kind of affinity].[12]

Drawing on Moacyr Garcia's comments about the existence of an initial

---

[10] See Luiz Costa Lima, 'A traição consequente ou a poesia de Cabral', in *Lira e antira: Mário, Drummond, Cabral* (Rio de Janeiro: Civilização Brasileira, 1968), pp. 237–410. See also Luiz Costa Lima, 'A lâmina assimétrica ou a ilusão da simetria', in *A metamorfose do silêncio* (Rio de Janeiro: Eldorado, 1974).

[11] I draw attention here especially to João Alexandre Barbosa's study *A imitação da forma: uma leitura de João Cabral de Melo Neto* (São Paulo: Duas Cidades, 1975).

[12] Othon Moacy Garcia, 'A página branca e o deserto', in *Esfinge clara e outros enigmas*, 2nd ed (Rio de Janeiro: Topbooks, 1996).

idea, a unique matrix, in his understanding of Cabral's limited repertoire of images in constant movement and organized according a sense of affinity (or even contrast), there does indeed appear to be a quite clear play between control and interference which seems to define Cabral's work especially after the 1950s. We might add to this Costa Lima's views on a process of internal tension within Cabral's series of images, and even the process identified by Barbosa of composition as being underpinned by a movement of intensification. With this in mind, it will not be difficult to verify that this poetic method really only takes shape in O cão sem plumas (1950) and becomes more defined in poems such as 'Uma faca só lâmina' (1956), which seems to function as a mechanism by which images are constructed through processes of confrontation and shifting relationships as necessary.

It may be possible, however, to add a feature to this process of image construction in Cabral's work: the figure of tangency, through which Leiris examined the practice of bullfighting, although it necessarily should be considered in the context not of the bullfight itself but of poetic practice. Leiris's essay, in fact, begins with considerations outside of bullfighting, thinking in terms of 'knots' and 'critical points', 'crossroads' and 'places where man touches the world and his own self'.[13] Only then, does Leiris move on to discuss bullfighting, as occupying places such as these. And as the 'figure itself of the union of opposites' (and not a simple 'association of contrasts') in which converge the beauty of calculated geometrical evolutions, of science, of technique, as well as relations based on contact, friction, imminent threat of catastrophe, announced by the coming closer of the bull. According to Leiris, what guides the bullfight, however, is not the simple contrast or opposition of these two tendencies, since this would not be enough, in his view.

Indeed, he identifies a kind of tangency, an almost-tangency, given that complete tangency would have catastrophic consequences. Instead, he speaks of convergences followed by divergences and shifts, of minimum avoidances and disconnections. When contact becomes evident, this should be 'avoided by a whisker', as though 'there were geometry, with disobedience', as though there were 'a constant twisting of such geometry'. Thus the moves by the bullfighter would necessarily reach 'somewhere halfway between the geometrical rule and its destruction' (pp. 33–35). For Leiris, the beauty of bullfighting resides precisely 'in a disconnection, avoidance and dissonance' though the passes and though a series of substitutions, shifts, inversions and 'shifts in axis'.

More than a bullfighting notion of beauty, however, Leiris seems to deal with the disruption of 'our notion of beauty'. Beauty seems to constitute itself, then, as an 'aspect of a mistaken struggle, a union, or rather a tangency'. Indeed, Leiris underlines the fact that 'beauty will not emerge from the mere contact of contrasting elements, but through their very antagonism, the manner in which one confronts the other, leaving its mark, such as a wound or damage' (p. 28).

[13] See Michel Leiris, *Espelho da tauromaquia* (São Paulo: Cosac & Naify, 2001), pp. 11–13.

Or, as Cabral would conclude in *O cão sem plumas*: 'O que vive fere' [That which lives wounds] (p. 114).

With the image of tangency in mind, it is perhaps worth returning briefly to the comments by Costa Lima, Othon Moacyr Garcia and João Alexandre Barbosa on the manner in which imagery functions in Cabral's poetry. In fact, rereading Costa Lima, it might not be possible to speak, for example, of a complete breaking up, or dissolution, of chains of images in Cabral since in this way the tension within these or among contrasting sequences of images would be lost. Moreover, it does not seem possible to speak exclusively about affinities between series of images, as Moacyr Garcia does, since this loses sight of the necessary disaccord that allows compositions which are based on divergence and diversion. And more than processes of intensification, as highlighted by João Alexandre Barbosa, which would necessarily involve an internal logic of evolution, an *in crescendo*, of the method of composition — what appears to create intensity with Cabral's images is above all the persistence of active antagonisms, even within his narrative poems. This we see in the tension between the images of the river, the dog and the fruit which unfold, converge and diverge in *O cão sem plumas*, or the bullet, the clock and the knife with which — through a tangency that is always on the verge — the poem 'Uma faca só lâmina' is constructed.

More than image or composition, it is in fact dynamics that underpin Cabral's poetic method. Not only of figuration (by means of sequences of almost-tangencies), but of a writing device that operates in pairs, in series (where the almost-tangencies go beyond the images and include tensions between mirroring poems). Hence his interest in bullfighting, for the significance that confrontation has for it, around situations 'unstable and difficult'.[14] Indeed, as Cabral states in his essay on Joan Miró's art, nothing can ever be guessed or forgotten for there are always 'pequenas surpresas' [small surprises]. In this way, as in bullfighting, as in works which abandon harmony and balance, the journey simply has to be followed and this, he emphasizes, 'só pode realizar-se dinamicamente' [can only be carried out dynamically] (p. 705).

*Translated by Sara Brandellero*

---

[14] See Cabral's 1950 study, 'Joán Miró', in *Obra completa*, pp. 689–720 (p. 718).

# Tactics of Attraction: Saints, Pilgrims and Warriors in the Portuguese Reconquista

Jonathan Wilson

*University of Liverpool*

Instances of the participation of northern European crusader fleets in the Portuguese Reconquista in the twelfth and early thirteenth centuries have, in general, been considered chance events. With the notable exception of the run-up to the conquest of Lisbon in 1147,[1] virtually all commentators have largely dismissed these episodes as the result of opportunistic Portuguese efforts to persuade passing maritime crusaders, mostly greedy for plunder, to join in Portuguese attacks on Iberian-Muslim strongholds.[2]

This paper argues that, following the outstanding success of the 1147 conquest of Lisbon, which was achieved principally thanks to the participation of foreign crusaders, the Portuguese operated an identifiable and sustained policy in order to attract more of these warriors to the fight on their frontier with Islam. This previously overlooked stratagem involved the construction and promotion of certain saintly cults as one of its principal tactics and, in particular, the cult of St Vincent of Saragossa which began to develop in Lisbon in the second half of the twelfth century, being promulgated in tandem with the unfolding Portuguese Reconquista.

Since at least the early twelfth century, Iberians witnessed the regular passage of fleets carrying northern European crusaders along their coasts. From places including England, Denmark, Frisia, Flanders, Lower Saxony and North Rhineland, these maritime pilgrim-warriors, when making necessary supply-stops in Hispanic ports, could sometimes be persuaded, usually in exchange for plunder, to take temporary service under Iberian Christian monarchs for the

---

[1] Luís Gonzaga de Azevedo, *História de Portugal*, 6 vols (Lisbon: Bíblion, 1939–44), vol. IV (1944), pp. 47–48; Harold V. Livermore, 'The "Conquest of Lisbon" and its Author', *Portuguese Studies*, 6 (1990), 1–16; Jonathan Phillips, 'St Bernard of Clairvaux, the Low Countries and the Lisbon Letter of the Second Crusade', *The Journal of Ecclesiastical History*, 48.3 (1997), 485–97; José Mattoso, *Afonso Henriques* (Rio de Mouro: Círculo de Leitores, 2006), pp. 167–71; Joseph F. O'Callaghan, *Reconquest and Crusade in Medieval Spain* (Philadelphia: University of Pennsylvania Press, 2004), pp. 41–43; Alan Forey, 'The Siege of Lisbon and the Second Crusade', *Portuguese Studies*, 20 (2004), 1–13; Lucas Villegas-Aristizábal, 'Revisiting the Anglo-Norman Crusaders' Failed Attempt to Conquer Lisbon, c. 1142', *Portuguese Studies*, 29.1 (2013), 7–20.
[2] Phillips, 'St Bernard of Clairvaux', p. 492, note 44.

prosecution of the campaign against the Moors of al-Andalus.³ Where Portugal is concerned, the historiography highlights the three best-documented instances of this phenomenon, namely the 1147 conquest of Lisbon, the conquest of Silves in 1189 in the Iberian south (today's Algarve), and the conquest of Alcácer do Sal, about 100 km south of Lisbon on the Sado estuary, in 1217. The reason for the peculiar geography of the conquests, given the chronology, is the massive Almohad counter attack that followed the conquest of Silves and which in 1191 not only re-conquered the city but also drove the Portuguese frontier back to the Lisbon side of the Tagus.

This paper introduces some of the factors indicating that the Portuguese purposely strove to create a cultural and ideological environment propitious to the realization of these joint ventures and that they operated, at least after 1147, specific tactics for attracting passing crusaders to join in the war on the Portuguese-Andalusi frontier, with the preparations for the 1217 attack on Alcácer do Sal representing the pinnacle of this strategy.

The conquest of Lisbon massively expanded the territory of the new-born kingdom of Portugal and established the Portuguese southern frontier definitively along the line of the Tagus. It was in many ways key to the establishment of Portugal as an independent state,⁴ and one of the only Christian successes of the entire Second Crusade. Its achievement was due, in large part, to the participation of northern maritime crusaders: these hardy warriors supplied much needed extra manpower, extra naval support and technological and tactical know-how.

Certainly the effectiveness of northern help in the seizing of Lisbon was clear to King Afonso Henriques who lost no time in appointing as bishop of the city one of those very same crusaders, the Englishman Gilbert of Hastings. Afonso promptly sent him back to England to muster troops for a proposed attack on Seville. The attack never took place, but Gilbert's efforts did lead to the arrival of a fleet from England which, together with Afonso's forces, launched an early and unsuccessful attack on Alcácer do Sal. In addition, Afonso briskly apportioned lands to northerners who elected to stay in the kingdom, a measure that would secure the occupation and colonization of newly conquered territories and cement links between Portugal and northern Europe.⁵

However, there appears to have been a more ambitious and long-term scheme put into operation by Afonso Henriques in order to attract warriors to Portugal and, indeed, pilgrims and their lucrative trade. Afonso had only to

---

³ *The Conquest of Lisbon, De Expugnatione Lyxbonensi*, trans. by Charles Wendell David (New York: Columbia University Press, 2001), pp. 12–26.
⁴ José Mattoso, 'Dois séculos de vicissitudes políticas', in José Mattoso (ed.), *História de Portugal*, 8 vols (Lisbon: Editorial Estampa, 1994), vol. II, *A monarquia feudal (1096–1480)*, p. 78.
⁵ Pedro Picoito, 'O Rei, o Santo e a Cidade: o culto de São Vicente em Lisboa e o projecto político de Afonso Henriques', in Isabel Alçada Cardoso (ed.), *São Vicente, diácono e mártir* (Lisbon: Cabido da Sé de Lisboa, 2005), pp. 57–87 (p. 58). For a general assessment of the significance of the conquest of Lisbon, see Maria João Branco's excellent 'Introdução' in Aires A. Nascimento, *A conquista de Lisboa aos Mouros* (Lisbon: Vega, 2007), pp. 9–51.

cast his eyes a little to the north, to Santiago de Compostela in Galicia, to find a shining example of how a powerful patron saint could change one's fortunes. The newly re-established diocese of Lisbon was suffragan to the Metropolitan of Compostela and, of course, the strenuous promotion of the cult of Saint James by Archbishop Diego Gelmirez, who had died only recently, in 1140, would have been fresh in the Portuguese psyche. It is certainly interesting that a copy of the *Liber Sancti Jacobi*, the book compiled probably under Gelmirez's direction, promulgating St James and the pilgrimage to Compostela, appeared during the second half of the twelfth century in the library of the monastery of Alcobaça,[6] one of the most important Portuguese royal institutions of the time. The success of the cult of Saint James 'the Moor slayer', is well known and little need be said of it here, save to observe that in almost all of the instances of the passage of the northern fleets along the west coast of Iberia, there is hardly a single one that does not make the stop at Compostela so that respects can be paid at the apostle's shrine. But Saint James was attracting pilgrims and warriors to Galicia where there was no longer any frontier with the Moors. The task which fell to Afonso was of course to attract warriors specifically to the Portuguese frontier. True, the fleets might well be forced to stop at Lisbon in any event to take on supplies — indeed until the 1230s it was the last Christian port before the Mediterranean — but it was by no means a foregone conclusion that they could be persuaded to stay and fight, as the disagreements among the crusaders reported at Lisbon and Alcácer demonstrate.[7] Whilst Portuguese offers of plunder may have been a powerful motivating factor for some, there were many whose motivations were genuinely spiritual and for whom the efficient prosecution and fulfilment of the pilgrimage vow to go to Jerusalem was paramount. Certainly, a little extra sanctity in Lisbon would be useful in convincing doubters of the divinity of the Portuguese struggle.

In 1173, during a period of truce with the Almohads, a Christian search party was sent, probably by local Mozarabs, from Lisbon to the south-western extremity of the Peninsula to retrieve the remains of the fourth-century Christian martyr St Vincent of Saragossa, who had rested on the Cape that still bears his name, *Cabo de São Vicente*, since he had been translated there from Valencia in the 700s. The body was located, parcelled-up, and translated again, accompanied by wondrous ravens and other miraculous events, in a boat to Lisbon where, after being rapturously welcomed by the people and the clergy, it was entombed in a chapel in the Cathedral. Thus was realized an ambition that Afonso Henriques had harboured certainly since some years previous to his conquest of Lisbon when he himself had made a premature and unsuccessful attempt to retrieve the martyr.[8]

[6] Lisbon, Biblioteca Nacional de Portugal, MS Alc. 334.
[7] David, *De Expugnatione Lyxbonensi*, pp. 101–11; Aires Augusto Nascimento, 'Poema de Conquista: a tomada de Alcácer do Sal aos Mouros (1217)', in *Poesía Latin Medieval (Siglos V-XV)* (Florence: SISMEL, 2005), pp. 619–37 (p. 634); Reinhold Röhricht (ed.), *Quinti Belli Sacri Scriptores Minores* (Geneva: Soc. De l'Or.Lat., 1879), pp. 62–63.
[8] Aires Augusto Nascimento and Saul António Gomes, *S. Vicente de Lisboa e seus milagres medievais*

In his desire for a patron saint, Afonso was following previous Christian princes of the Reconquista who had translated to their northern territories the bodies of important saints from the Islamic south; ample precedent resided in the translation of St Eulogius from Cordoba to Oviedo in 883 by Alfonso III of Asturias, and the translation of St Isidore from Seville to León in 1063 by Fernando the Great. Now like Oviedo in León, Toledo in Castile and of course Compostela in Galicia, Lisbon in Portugal was now to possess its own renowned saintly relics.

The account of Vincent's translation was set in writing shortly after the event by Estêvão, cantor of Lisbon Cathedral, in his *Miracula Sancti Vincentii*. Estêvão is very clear on Vincent's relocation in establishing the status of the city telling us that 'by this act of heavenly grace [Lisbon...] can be considered above the cities in its vicinity.'[9] Estêvão then goes on to enumerate the miracles associated with St Vincent, not forgetting the Reconquista since, featured in the miracle stories are Gualdim Pais, Master of the Templars, and Gonçalo Viegas, governor of Portuguese Estremadura, future founder of the Military Order of Évora.[10]

At first blush Vincent seems a strange choice for Portugal's favourite saint, since he was not at all Portuguese. According to his tradition, largely repeated by Estêvão, he had been deacon to the Bishop of Saragossa and was martyred in 304 by the Roman prefect Dacian. Having been imprisoned in Valencia he underwent various grisly tortures and when offered his freedom on condition that he burn the Scriptures he refused and was martyred. After his death, ravens protected his corpse from being eaten by wild animals until his companions arrived to retrieve the body. In the second half of the eighth century his body was rescued from Valencia, the city having come under Muslim attack, and translated to Cape St Vincent where a shrine was established, which was watched over by ever-present miraculous ravens.[11]

Why choose the Spanish saint, Vincent, as the patron saint of Lisbon? There were other candidates closer to home. At the time of the 1147 conquest, Lisbon contained a flourishing community of Mozarabs with its own tradition of saints martyred in the city during the time of Dacian, for example, Saints Veríssimus, Máxima and Júlia, among several others.[12] Yet there is no evidence that a Vincent cult had existed in the city — at least there appears to have been no church in his dedication. There was some devotion to Vincent in other parts

(Lisbon: Edições Didaskalia, 1988), pp. 30–31. Pedro Picoito has made a persuasive case for the retrieval of St Vincent in 1173 being the initiative, not of Afonso Henriques, but of the disgruntled Mozarabs of the city unhappy about the suppression of their liturgy in favour of the Roman rite promoted by the conquerors: 'A trasladação de S. Vicente, consenso e conflito na Lisboa do século XII', *Medievalista online*, 4.4 (2008). <http://www2.fcsh.unl.pt/iem/medievalista/MEDIEVALISTA4/medievalista-picoito.htm> [accessed 17 February 2014].
[9] Nascimento and Gomes, *S. Vicente de Lisboa*, pp. 40–41. English trans. by the author.
[10] Ibid., p. 14.
[11] For a comprehensive study of the Portuguese cult of St Vincent, see Isabel Rosa Dias, *Culto e memória textual de S. Vicente em Portugal (da Idade Média ao século XVI)* (Faro: Universidade do Algarve, 2003, revised Lisbon, 2011).
[12] Nascimento and Gomes, *S. Vicente de Lisboa*, p. 9; Picoito, 'A Trasladação', p. 1.

of twelfth-century Portugal, but a survey of the churches consecrated to him shows that his cult was of only very moderate popularity compared to those of Stª Maria, St Salvador, St Martin of Tours or the apostles St James and St Peter. So popularity was clearly not the most important contributing factor.[13]

Rather the appeal of Vincent for the Portuguese seems to have been his popularity north of the Pyrenees and particularly in France where, from the Merovingian period onwards, his cult had enjoyed an impressive prominence, as is demonstrated by a substantial number of surviving texts. Among them the *Liber Historiae Francorum* and the *Vita Droctovei Abbatis* relating how King Childebert, when besieging Saragossa in 541, obtained the martyr's stole from the bishop of the city. Returning to Paris, Childebert founded the basilica of St Vincent, later dedicated to Saint-Germain-des-Prés, where the relic was housed. There are also later accounts of expeditions of various French clerics to Spain in search of more relics of the Saint, including those in the ninth century of Usuard, also from Saint-Germain-des-Prés, and the monk Audald of the monastery of Conques, and that of Herman of Laon following the Christian conquest of Saragossa in 1118.[14] Reports of centres dedicated to the cult of Vincent in France are numerous. Gregory of Tours mentions several churches founded in the sixth century that were dedicated to him, some containing relics.[15] Meanwhile, at the liturgical level, accounts of the Passion of Vincent circulated in France from an early period, transmitted in various texts with the poem included in Prudentius' *Peristephanon* being the earliest.[16]

It is probable that knowledge in Portugal of the cult of Vincent north of the Pyrenees received a substantial boost with the increasing settlement of French clerics and knights during the eleventh and twelfth centuries, largely on the back of the Romano-Cluniac reform famously encouraged by Alfonso VI of Castile-León. However, in the present context, most interesting is the popularity that Iberian saints enjoyed in Flanders and Belgium. Rainer II of Hainaut went to Spain in 986 where, having aided the Castilians in the Reconquista, he received in recompense, in the city of Oviedo, the relics of St Leocadia (patron saint of Toledo). These were housed in the important Benedictine monastery of Saint-Ghislain in Hainaut which, along with the nearby Abbey of Saint Amand, appears to have maintained relations with St Salvador in Oviedo, both of these Flemish monasteries possessing copies made in their own *scriptoria* of manuscripts from St Salvador, and with the library of Saint-Ghislain containing texts on St Leocádia and several on St Vincent himself.[17]

---

[13] Dias, *Culto e memória textual de S. Vicente*, pp. 75–92. <http://www.scribd.com/doc/125133247/Culto-e-Memoria-Textual-de-S-Vicente-texto-revisto> [accessed 17 February 2014]

[14] Dias, *Culto e memória textual de S. Vicente*, pp. 82–83; Nascimento and Gomes, *S. Vicente de Lisboa*, p. 9.

[15] On the popularity of the cult of St Vincent in France and Belgium, see Dias, *Culto e memória textual de S. Vicente*, pp. 82–85.

[16] *The Poems of Prudentius*, trans. by M Clement Eagan, in Fathers of The Church Series, vol. 43, (Washington, DC: C.U.A. Press, 1962) pp. 146–67.

[17] Dias, *Culto e memória textual de S. Vicente*, pp. 83, note 127.

Moving on to the period of the Third Crusade, it is following Hattin in 1187, and the call to the Third Crusade, that we really start to see evidence of the Portuguese truly grasping the nettle. They know by now, full well, that a whole series of well-armed Northern flotillas are going to be passing their coasts imminently, so they pull out all the stops to attract them to join in the fight against the Iberian Saracens. The sticking-point is that there is still a considerable amount of doubt among the crusaders as to the spiritual worthiness of the fight in Iberia, compared with the fight in the Holy Land. Evidence for this is abundant in the sources for all three events, particularly at Lisbon and Alcácer where various contingents of crusaders dispute between them whether to accept Portuguese invitations to join campaigns, or whether to abandon operations when sieges drag on.[18]

To get around this, the Portuguese strove to imbue their Reconquista with as much divine favour as possible, firstly, by boosting the sanctity of Lisbon and, secondly, by ramming home to crusaders the notion that if they fell in battle in Iberia, a martyr's crown awaited them in heaven. Happily, St Vincent was already in place, and had been generally inflating the holiness of Lisbon and boosting its international profile for well over a decade. We do not know exactly when Estêvão wrote his *Miracula Sancti Vincentii*, but it may well have been in about 1187/88, when it suddenly became urgent to fix the martyr's connection with the city in writing. Next, to address the sanctity of the war on the Muslims of Iberia, in the year 1188, one year after Hattin and one year before King Sancho's daring conquest of Silves, an anonymous author penned the *Indiculum Fundationis Monasterii Beati Vincentii Vlixbone* and helpfully included the date of redaction in his text.[19] Whilst ostensibly recounting the story of the foundation of the Lisbon monastery of S. Vicente da Fora, a house dedicated to the Saint without ever housing his relics, the *Indiculum* is a text acutely concerned with drawing together a number of themes designed to address all the concerns a doubting crusader might have over the worthiness of the Portuguese war on the Saracens.[20]

In the prologue, the author emphasizes the veracity of his text. He tells us that he has taken his account from the direct oral testimony of two veterans of the conquest of Lisbon, one a Portuguese nobleman, the other, significantly, a German named Otto who had chosen to stay in Portugal and entered the

---

[18] *The Conquest of Lisbon*, pp. 101-11; Charles Wendell David (ed.), *Narratio de Itinere Navali Peregrinorum Hierosolymam Tendentium et Silviam Capientium, AD 1189* in *Proceedings, American Philosophical Society* 81 (1939), 591-678 (pp. 627-29); Nascimento, 'Poema de Conquista', p. 634, lines 87-90, and p. 635, lines 123-26.

[19] Aires A. Nascimento (ed. and trans.), *Indiculum Fundationis Monasterii Beati Vincentii Vlixbone*, in *A Conquista de Lisboa aos Mouros*, pp. 178-81.

[20] Although arriving at differing conclusions, the author acknowledges a debt of gratitude to two important treatments of aspects of the *Indiculum*; Stephen Lay, 'Miracles, Martyrs and the Cult of Henry the Crusader in Lisbon', *Portuguese Studies*, 24.1 (2008), 7-31; and Armando Sousa Pereira, 'Guerra e santidade: o cavaleiro-mártir Henrique de Bona e a conquista cristã de Lisboa', *Lusitania Sacra*, 2ª série, 17 (2005), 15-38.

royal monastery of Santa Cruz de Coimbra. Immediately following this short introduction, the *Indiculum* launches straight into its main concern. Within just a few lines, we are left in no doubt, not only as to the heroic nature of the German warriors but, crucially, that those who fell in Christian battle at the siege of Lisbon wear the crown of martyrdom.[21] To prove this is so, the *Indiculum* recounts the occurrence of miraculous events during the battle for the city. For the most part they take place in the cemetery for German and Flemish dead established by the crusaders; this site shortly afterwards became the location upon which was built the monastery of S. Vicente da Fora. The miracles in the cemetery happen at the tomb of a Germanic crusader of Cologne, one Henry who is, we are told, a knight of noble lineage and character, born at Bonn, who dies in battle some days before Lisbon is conquered. First of all, two youths, standing guard at the tomb, both deaf and mute from birth, are healed after having been visited at night by the dead Henry bearing a palm branch. The palm branch of course is highly symbolic, not only of martyrdom but also of pilgrimage; two themes the *Indiculum* is very keen to link. Next, Henry-of-Bonn's squire is killed and, in the chaos of battle, is buried at a location in the cemetery somewhat distant from his master's tomb. Henry appears in dreams to the night watchman and urges him to retrieve the body of his squire and place it in the tomb next to him. This is done, the night watchman, though terrified, proclaiming that in the performance of the arduous act of disinterment and reburial, he miraculously experienced no fatigue whatsoever.[22]

Another miracle happens when communion bread shared out to crusaders at the daily mass bleeds as it is cut. This is caused by the bread having been made from the stolen flour that a dying crusader had bequeathed to the poor. Within this miracle is the implicit proof that the dying crusader who made the bequest is now a martyr in heaven.[23]

These miracles are proclaimed throughout the Christian camp and Henry-of-Bonn is hailed a true martyr of Christ, whereupon the Christian forces, filled with divine inspiration, renew their efforts and win the city.

Galvanizing as this tale may be, the *Indiculum* is not content to stop there. Shortly after the conquest, the miracles around Henry's tomb begin again. It is here that the *Indiculum* shows its profound preoccupation with linking the two all-important themes, that of martyrdom in battle in Iberia and that of the Jerusalem Pilgrimage. In this, the *Indiculum* seeks to address directly the major conceptual obstacle that appears to have existed for many crusaders when faced with the prospect of campaigning in Iberia and which arises essentially from the preaching of Urban II and the First Crusade. This obstacle resides in the immensely powerful pull in the popular imagination of the physical city of

---

[21] Nascimento, *A Conquista de Lisboa*, pp. 178–81; Lay, 'Miracles, Martyrs and the Cult of Henry', p. 20; Pereira, 'Guerra e santidade', p. 22.
[22] *Indiculum*, pp. 184–87
[23] Ibid., pp. 186–87.

Jerusalem and the Holy Land, in literal notions of the *imitatio Christi*, and of taking up Christ's cross in the land 'where His feet have stood'.²⁴ The crucial point is that because of a very Jerusalem-centric interpretation of the crusading vow, for many crusaders, the true Christian fight could not take place anywhere other than in Palestine. The device which the *Indiculum* introduces to solve the problem is a heavenly palm tree which miraculously comes into being at Henry-of-Bonn's tomb. We are told:

> It was the case that a palm branch, which had been brought on the shoulders of pilgrims from Jerusalem according to the custom, having been placed on the tomb at the head of the martyr, shortly thereafter grew green again, rose up out of the ground and grew in height so that it became a tree covered in leaves of fresh green. Now, all those that had illnesses came to that tomb in order to make their supplications and, taking [a leaf] from the palm, they hung it around their neck or, reducing it to a powder, drank it and immediately they were cured of any disease that might be afflicting them.²⁵

The image of the palm tree appears to serve at least three functions. In the first place, it is miraculous and confirms the continuing status of Henry as a martyr. Secondly, the palm branch itself, which is also carried by Henry in his appearance to the two deaf-mutes, is traditionally symbolic of his status as a martyr. This is not peculiar to Henry, of course, but here we have his martyrdom doubly confirmed! Thirdly, and most importantly here, is that the palm is symbolic of the pilgrimage to Jerusalem. Crusaders visiting Jerusalem often brought a palm branch back home with them, as proof they had completed their pilgrimage and fulfilled their vow, from where we get the name 'palmers' often used to describe returning crusaders.²⁶ It is here that the notion of the *Iter per Hispaniam*, or 'Route through Spain', becomes highly relevant.²⁷ Notably, Archbishop Diego Gelmirez of Santiago de Compostela appears to have been among the first to enunciate the principle at a Council in Compostela; the *Historia Compostellana* records his formulation as follows:

> Just as the soldiers of Christ and faithful sons of the holy Church opened up the way to Jerusalem with much blood, so let us prove ourselves to be soldiers of Christ and, having vanquished his most wicked enemies, the Saracens, let us also, with the help of His grace, open up a way to that same sepulchre of the Lord through the region of Spain, which is shorter and much less laborious.²⁸

---

²⁴ See William J. Purkis's incisive exposition of the 'conceptual problem' facing foreign crusaders in Iberia arising from preponderant emphasis on the Jerusalem pilgrimage in *Crusading Spirituality in the Holy Land and Iberia, c.1095-c.1187* (Woodbridge: Boydell Press, 2008), especially pp. 125–38.
²⁵ Nascimento, *A Conquista de Lisboa aos Mouros*, p. 193. English trans. by the author.
²⁶ James A. Brundage, *Medieval Canon Law and the Crusader* (Madison: University of Wisconsin Press, 1969), pp. 124–25.
²⁷ Purkis, *Crusading Spirituality in the Holy Land*, p. 131 et seq.
²⁸ E. Falque Rey (ed.), *Historia Compostellana* in *Corpus Christianorum, Continuatio Mediaevalis* vol. LXX (Turnhout: Brepols, 1988), pp. 379–80. English trans. by the author.

His words have caused some problems since it is difficult to see how the passage through Spain (and then presumably across North Africa and up through Egypt) could be 'shorter' and 'less laborious' than the land passage through eastern Europe and Constantinople. Whether he may have been referring to the sea passage rather than the land journey, or indeed to both passage by land and sea, which would be more likely, his overriding aim appears to have been to bring Iberia unequivocally within the ideological ambit of the pilgrimage to Jerusalem.[29]

The *Iter per Hispaniam* most famously struck a chord with Alfonso I 'the Battler' of Aragon-Navarre who was much taken with the Jerusalem-centric notion of crusading, more so than his Iberian peers. Following his conquest of Saragossa in 1118, over the next couple of years he extended his territory well south of the Ebro. Needing to protect his new conquests, he established two military confraternities, that of Belchite and that of Monreal, inspired probably by the Order of the Temple. Both had the stated purpose, either expressly in their Rule or specified in the wording of indulgences granted to them, of opening 'the road to Jerusalem from this region [of Spain]'.[30] It is notable that the emblem of the confraternity of Belchite appears to have been a palm tree according to a passage from Orderic Vitalis where they are described as the *Fratres de Palmis* or 'Brothers of the Palm'.[31] Significant here is Purkis's analysis of the likely significance of the palm tree for the members of the confraternity of Belchite, given their mandate and given the significance of the palm for the Jerusalem pilgrimage; namely that they perceived the palm tree as an emblem of their mission to carve a path through Spain to the Holy City.[32] Could it be that we have a similar use of palm tree imagery in the *Indiculum* and in the cult of Henry-of-Bonn? Was the palm tree of Lisbon, miraculously grown up from a branch from Jerusalem, presented as proof of the sacred fusion of the principles of martyrdom-in-Iberia and the Jerusalem Pilgrimage? Was it used as a powerful and readily understood motif intended to assuage the doubts of crusaders less interested in plunder and more interested in their crusading vow?

This conceptual problem of the Jerusalem pilgrimage appears to have been well known to King Sancho I and he knew that, because of it, he would have little chance of involving crusaders in a campaign inland. As Herculano suggested, Sancho's preferred target in 1189 would most likely have been Juromenha, some 200 km east of Lisbon, in order to push his frontier to the River Guadiana and support Évora, a vulnerable outpost far from the banks of the Tagus. Instead he

---

[29] Cf., Patrick J. O'Banion, 'What has Iberia to do with Jerusalem? Crusade and the Spanish Route to the Holy Land in the Twelfth Century,' *Journal of Medieval History*, 34.4 (2008), 383–95. There is some evidence that the passage over land was perceived by certain contemporaries as an easy option; see TSRB 'Untitled Review,' *The English Historical Review*, 57.227 (July 1942), 394–95.

[30] O'Banion, 'What has Iberia to do with Jerusalem?', pp. 388–89. See also p. 392, where it is suggested that the charter of union of the Order of Santiago includes the *Iter per Hispaniam* principle.

[31] *The Ecclesiastical History of Orderic Vitalis*, vol. VI, trans. by Marjorie Chibnall (Oxford: Clarendon Press, 1978), p. 400.

[32] Purkis, *Crusading Spirituality in the Holy Land*, p. 135.

was forced to focus his efforts in the south, on the important Almohad naval base at Silves, if he were to have any chance of taking advantage of the valuable military support coming his way. His plan seems to have been to try to create a frontier which ran from Silves to Beja and then to Évora — supporting Évora from the south. He then presumably hoped to move on Juromenha at a later stage.[33] This, of course, did not happen thanks to the terrific Almohad counter offensive of 1190–91.

Moving forward in time to the run-up to the Fifth Crusade and the 1217 conquest of Alcácer do Sal, the principal architect of the conquest was Soeiro Viegas, the incumbent Bishop of Lisbon. Soeiro is a controversial figure about whom the lacunae in the documentary record frequently leave us guessing; however, sufficient information does emerge to suggest his involvement in a substantial campaign of forward-planning in the assembly of the forces necessary to take Alcácer. This port-town was a fearsomely well-fortified Almohad stronghold near the open sea on the right bank of the Sado, and very convenient indeed for maritime crusaders anxious to minimise delays to their Jerusalem pilgrimage. In addition, Alcácer was the strategic gateway to the Christian conquest of the Andalusi south.

Yet, aside from the prosecution of the Portuguese fight against the infidel, there were other important reasons why Alcácer would have seemed like a good idea at the time. In the first place Afonso II needed a military victory, and particularly a victory against the Muslims. He had succeeded to the Portuguese throne in 1211 on the death of his father, Sancho I, and appears to have suffered from a life-long physical condition, possibly leprosy, which kept him from direct participation in military endeavours. If prevailing contemporary attitudes generally equated military prowess with royal legitimacy, then the situation in Portugal was acute. Afonso Henriques, Afonso II's grandfather, had in 1179 finally won papal recognition of his kingship almost exclusively thanks to a lifetime of successful campaigns against the Muslims. This kingship had been confirmed to Sancho I in 1190, following his conquest of Silves the previous year. Afonso II could show none of these martial qualities and he had signally failed to participate in the great Christian victory at Las Navas de Tolosa in 1212. Even if he had been physically capable of presenting himself at Las Navas, he was at the time locked into a serious legal dispute with his sisters, the *Infantas*, over his father Sancho's will, which had alienated to them large swathes of strategic Portuguese territory. King Alfonso IX of León, taking advantage of the crisis, had invaded Northern Portugal in support of the *Infantas*, precipitating splits in the Portuguese nobility and a short civil war. Essentially, a timely military triumph over the Muslims would consolidate Afonso II's power, wining him favour among his nobility and in Rome.[34]

---

[33] Alexandre Herculano, *Histόra de Portugal*, vol. 1 (Lisbon: Bertrand Editora, 2007), pp. 410–28.
[34] On Afonso II of Portugal see Herminia Vasconcellos Vilar, *D. Afonso II, Um Rei Sem Tempo* (Rio de Mouro: Círculo de Leitores, 2006). Whilst it is scarcely conceivable that the campaign that led to the

Bishop Soeiro of Lisbon, meanwhile, had his own reasons for wanting a victory. Rising to the episcopal throne in 1211, he was soon to become embroiled in disputes both inside and outside his diocese, the details of which have remained unclear. On top of these quarrels, Soeiro's relations with Innocent III appear to have been far from rosy, since the Pope had conducted certain inquiries into alleged irregularities in the bishop's conduct. One thing at least seems sure enough: in the early years of his episcopate, Soeiro was the target of considerable hostility.[35] In short, he needed a personal triumph to improve his standing with several groups and institutions, perhaps not least with the Pope.

Certainly as early as 1213, Soeiro would have seen a great opportunity coming his way when the venture later known as the Fifth Crusade was announced.[36] Further, the proclamation, also in 1213, of the Fourth Lateran Council, scheduled for two years later, not only gave Pope Innocent ample time to make his plans and preparations, but also afforded the very same to Soeiro Viegas, who held his own bishopric only thanks to the efforts of northern crusaders on their way by sea to the East. His anticipation was no doubt powerfully fuelled by the early successes of Oliver of Paderborn who had been preaching the crusade in the Low Countries. In a letter to the Count of Namur in only June of 1214, Oliver reports that a great number of pilgrims, some 50,000, had enlisted for the Crusade, '8,000 equipped with shields or breast plates, 1,000 wearing a cuirass.' He adds, 'Know also that there are disposed so many ships to participate in the expedition of Jesus Christ that I believe just from the province of Cologne will come more than 300 [ships], perfectly equipped with warriors, weapons, arms, victuals and other warlike accoutrements.'[37]

Of course Oliver would be present at the Fourth Lateran Council in 1215, along with so many other churchmen, the lengthy two-year period of notice leading up to the council serving to ensure maximum attendance. Indeed, the council which met in November 1215 was the largest assembly of ecclesiastical hierarchy ever convened during the Medieval period.[38] Such unprecedented attendance would have been anticipated by Soeiro who, both through his direct personal relations and through his associates, always remained in close touch with prevailing attitudes in Rome. In view of the dazzling opportunities presented by the Council for the furtherance of his plans, we can have little doubt that he placed it at the very heart of his strategy. We know he attended along with the other Portuguese prelates including leaders of the Alcácer campaign such as the Abbot of Alcobaça, the Bishop of Évora and the Master of the Temple-

conquest of Alcácer could have taken place without the full knowledge and support of Afonso II, the extent of his involvement in preparations for the enterprise is unknown; see Vilar, pp. 137–38.

[35] Maria João Branco, 'Reis, bispos e cabidos: a diocese de Lisboa durante o primeiro século da sua restauração', in *Lusitania Sacra*, 2ª série, 10 (1998), 70–84.

[36] James M. Powell, *Anatomy of a Crusade, 1213–1221* (Philadelphia: University of Pennsylvania Press, 1990), pp. 15–17.

[37] Oliver of Paderborn, *Die Schriften des Kölner Domscholasters*, ed. by H. Hoogeweg (Tübingen: Litterarischer Verein, 1894), pp. 285–86. English trans. by the author.

[38] Powell, *Anatomy of a Crusade*, pp. 33–50.

in-Iberia.³⁹ We do not know to whom Soeiro spoke at the council, but we can compile a list of suspects simply by looking at the geography of the lands of origin of the personnel usually making up the northern fleets: the high-clergy of Cologne, we could suppose, perhaps including Oliver of Paderborn, and the abbots and priors of the major religious institutions in Lower Saxony and the Low Countries. We know that the Portuguese fight against Islam was high on Soeiro's agenda since it is reported by fellow-attendee, the Frisian Abbot Emón, that the bishop went as far as to ask Innocent III directly for permission for expeditionary troops to fight in Portugal, a request that was refused, although there is no evidence this stopped Soeiro canvassing support for his design.⁴⁰

Who did Soeiro take along with him from his chapter at Lisbon, given that it was certainly that Portuguese diocese that could be expected to gain significant, and more or less immediate, material benefits from the conquest of Alcácer? One likely member of Soeiro's diplomatic team was cantor of Lisbon, Fernando Peres. He was of a wealthy family, well educated in law, probably at Bologna, and a high profile operator in royal and ecclesiastical politics.⁴¹ But, besides his general *curriculum vitae*, two further points support his presence at the Fourth Lateran Council. Firstly he, like Soeiro, disappears from the diocesan documentation during the period of the Council. Secondly, there arises at this time another account of the translation of St Vincent to Lisbon, intriguingly from the library of the monastery of Saint-Ghislain in Hainaut in Belgium. The so-called *Relatio de Translatione Sancti Vincentii Martyris*,⁴² conventionally dated to the early thirteenth century, relates a version of the story in large part from the oral testimony, according to the prologue, of a certain 'archdeacon' of the Cathedral of Lisbon, one Fernando who is described as 'a venerable man both through divine religion and lineage'.

Written probably by a monk of Saint-Ghislain, one immediately striking feature of the *Relatio* is that it is abundant in details concerning the Portuguese historical context of the translation of St Vincent to Lisbon, including: the approximate date of the translation; that Afonso Henriques was king at the time; that Pope Alexander III had granted him the title of King; that the crusaders of northern Europe had laboured in the conquest of Lisbon; and that the tomb of St Vincent in the Cathedral of Lisbon had been endowed with rich ornamental decoration on royal orders.⁴³ At this point, the text makes explicit reference to Princess Matilda, daughter of Afonso Henriques, who in 1184 had married Philip of Alsace, Count of Flanders and who, following Philip's death at the siege of Acre in 1191, had stayed in Flanders. The *Relatio* recounts how,

---

³⁹ Denis Jean Achille Luchaire, 'Un document retrouvé', in *Journal des Savants*, 3 (1905), 557–68.
⁴⁰ *Quinti Belli Sacri Scriptores Minores*, p. 63.
⁴¹ Maria José Azevedo Santos, *Vida e morte de um mosteiro cisterciense* (Lisbon: Edições Colibri, 1998), pp. 55–63.
⁴² Brussels: Biblioteca Real da Bélgica, MS Códice II. 981, fols 100ᵛ–104ʳ.
⁴³ See Dias, *Culto e memória*, Apêndice IV, pp. 207–20 for reproduction of Latin text and Portuguese translation.

on the closing of the tomb of St Vincent with ugly iron grills in order to protect it from attackers, Afonso Henriques and his daughter Matilda ordered that the bars be covered with silver and gold and precious stones. This contrasts sharply with the texts making up the Portuguese tradition of the translation of St Vincent, which attribute the adornment of the bars exclusively to Afonso Henriques. It would appear then that the monk-author of Saint-Ghislain is lauding the memory of Matilda Countess of Flanders. But, if this reference is to be considered a Portuguese tactic of attracting northerners by highlighting the links between the Low Countries and Portugal, why does Cantor Fernando not similarly invoke the other Portuguese royal with Flemish connections of more recent memory, Matilda's nephew Prince Fernando, the younger brother of King Afonso II?

Prince Fernando had, by marriage in 1212, become Count of Flanders; however, his essentially disastrous rule saw war between Flanders and France, his defeat at the Battle of Bouvines and his subsequent imprisonment by Philip Augustus in 1214. All this appears to have tarnished the Portuguese reputation in Flanders.[44] However, if Fernando's memory was best left uncelebrated, the appeal to the memory of his aunt, a long-time resident of Flanders, was apparently still worthwhile. And if her Christianity was in doubt, here we have her Christian orthodoxy reinstated in the *Relatio* through the explicit record of her active participation in the translation of St Vincent. Of course, we may suppose that Fernando Peres spoke of St Vincent and his translation to Lisbon in similar terms to other religious besides the anonymous monk-author of Saint-Ghislain. Probably the reason for our finding a written record of Fernando's mission in that particular monastery is that Saint-Ghislain already had an interest in the cult of St Vincent and thus it would have been more pressing in that institution, as opposed to others with lesser links to the cult, to fix Fernando's message in textual form as a valuable addition to the collection of Vincentiana already present in the monastery.

Further evidence of these Portuguese tactics of attraction emerges in a passage from the contemporary chronicle of the aforementioned Abbot Emón, of the Frisian Premonstratensian house of Floridus Hortus, the very same text that informs us of Soeiro's request at the Lateran Council to Innocent III for crusader aid in Portugal along the way. Far from being deterred by Innocent's refusal, there is evidence that Soeiro may have redoubled his efforts, especially where the Frisians were concerned; it is a matter for speculation whether a certain Frisian reluctance to participate in his plan had emerged during the Council. Abbot Emón, in the Chronicle of his Abbey,[45] reproduces the report of an unnamed member of his household who had sailed with the Frisian squadron that arrived in Lisbon in 1217. The Frisians refused to take part in

---

[44] Louis Gonzaga de Azevedo, *História de Portugal*, 6 vols (Lisbon: Bíblion, 1940–42), vol. v, pp. 122–26; Stephen Lay, *The Reconquest Kings of Portugal* (Basingstoke: Palgrave Macmillan, 2009), pp. 213–14.

[45] *Cronica Floridi Horti*, Groningen: Universiteitsbibliotheek, MS 116.

the conquest of Alcácer, splitting off from the rest of the fleet and carrying on their voyage to Palestine. Nevertheless, the report, edited by Röhricht as the *De Itinere Frisonum*,[46] contains an account of the state of the tomb of the martyr Henry-of-Bonn in Lisbon in 1217:

> To the east, outside the city, is found the venerable monastery where presently is seen the lofty palm tree which grows from the tomb of the martyr-of-Christ, Popteto Uluinga, a chief of the Christian soldiery who, having changed his name to that of Henry, ended his life in Christ in this same place seventy years ago, along with his squire; and who, now canonized by divine revelation, enjoys temporal and eternal glory.[47]

Several notable points arise from this passage. In the first place, according to the *Indiculum* written in 1188 which is the earliest mention of the miraculous palm tree, the tree has already disappeared, either removed to another location, or destroyed because so many pilgrims took pieces of it for the cure of their ailments.[48] Now, miraculously enough, in 1217 it is suddenly back for all to see. Does this represent special preparations in Lisbon in 1217 for the boosting of Henry's cult which might include the convenient re-appearance of the palm tree? Also we note that the Frisian source relates that Henry was originally called Popteto Uluinga. Where does this information come from? The tradition of Henry, first reported in the *Indiculum*, appears to be an entirely Portuguese phenomenon, but now we have this added detail. Could it be that this information was communicated to the author of the Frisian report through an oral tradition when he arrived in Lisbon, or could it have been imparted to him earlier, say at the Fourth Lateran Council? We do not know, of course. However, in the *Gesta Frisiorum*, a later chronicle of Frisian deeds dating to the mid-fourteenth century, we learn that among the Frisians at Lisbon in 1217 was one Popteto, 'a man of mature age and admirable piety' from Wirdum.[49] Two places are named Wirdum in the north-eastern Netherlands. So now Henry/Popteto is not German at all, but Frisian! Sure enough, in the *Gesta*, Popteto valiantly leads his troops into battle, exhorting them to Christian martyrdom. But when the victory is won and Lisbon is rescued, Popteto is killed by a Saracen sniper's arrow, whereupon he himself enters heaven a martyr. Above his tomb in Lisbon, a beautiful and miraculous palm-tree appears, which the Lisboans perceive as a great wonder. The *Gesta*, although from the fourteenth century, appears to be inspired by other legends regarding Henry/Popteto whose provenance is difficult to divine and we can only imagine how much may be owed to oral traditions that circulated in Lisbon in 1217.[50]

[46] *Quinti Belli Sacri Scriptores Minores*, pp. 59–70.
[47] Ibid., p. 62. English trans. by the author.
[48] Nascimento, *A Conquista de Lisboa aos Mouros*, pp. 192–93.
[49] E. Epkema and J. W. de Crane (eds.), *Oude Friesche kronijken. Uitgegeven door net Friesch Genootschap* (Leeuwarden: G. T. N. Suringar, 1853), pp. 283–306.
[50] Cf. Jaime Ferreiro Alemparte, *Arribas de Normandos y Cruzados a las Costas de la Península Ibérica* (Madrid: Sociedad Española de Estudios Medievales, 1999), pp. 158–59.

Fig. 1. Bishop Soeiro's sarcophagus in Lisbon Cathedral: note the palm tree carving

Certainly the palm motif seems to have been important to Bishop Soeiro. He died in 1233 and his sarcophagus is found in a cloister-chapel, in Lisbon Cathedral. Although his career was long and eventful, it appears to have been above all for his conquest of Alcácer that he wished to be remembered (or for which he *was* remembered). The epitaph on his tomb is short and clear:

> Lord Suerius Bishop of Lisbon lies here who, during the reign of Afonso II, took Alcácer do Sal from the Moors in 1217.[51]

On the rough-hewn stone lid are just three simple carvings, all about the same size: a bishop's crosier, a cross and an unmistakable palm-tree.

If we can say that there are, broadly, three principal participant peoples making up the contingents of maritime Northern crusaders in the Portuguese Reconquista, that is, the Lower Rhinelanders, the Flemings, and the Frisians, then the Portuguese use similar tactics of attraction on all of them: the Lower Rhinelanders are given Henry-of-Bonn, the Frisians are given Popteto Uluinga, and the Flemings, in the library of Saint-Ghislain, receive their own special version of the translation of St Vincent to Lisbon. At the same time, appeal is made to each and every crusader, regardless of nationality, in the image of the miraculous palm tree.

Yet there exists a notable absence in this scheme of attraction. Did not the Anglo-Normans, a leading element in the momentous conquest of Lisbon, merit their own bespoke saintly allure in Portugal, over and above the generic

---

[51] [DOMNUS SUARIUS ULIXBO] | NEN[SIS E]PISCO[PUS HIC] | JACET;-QUI REGNANTE | ALFONSO 2º A MAURIS | ALCASSARUM SALIS | ERIPUIT; AN[NO] DE; [1217]; Mário Barroca, *Epigrafia Medieval Portuguesa*, 3 vols (Lisbon: Fundação Calouste Gulbenkian, 2000), vol. 2, book 1, pp. 745–46. English trans. by the author.

appeal of the palm tree? Indeed, they were not left out. Portuguese efforts in this direction were amply served in a spectacular way in 1170 when four knights loyal to Henry II of England entered Canterbury Cathedral on the night of 29 December and murdered Archbishop Thomas Becket at the high altar. By February 1173, Anglo-Norman Becket had officially become St Thomas with an already powerful and prospering cult.

Evidence for the early promotion of the cult of St Thomas in Portugal is strong. The very earliest known copy of the *Liber miraculorum beati Thome*, compiled by Benedict of Peterborough, exists among the manuscripts of Alcobaça copied from an earlier exemplar in the library of the important Portuguese Benedictine monastery of S. Mamede de Lorvão.[52] The colophon precisely dates the execution of the copy to 1185, with the Miracles being immediately followed in the same codex by a Passion of Thomas and a lost Becket letter the presence of which in Portugal, just twelve years after Becket's formal canonization, is remarkable and begs urgent explanation.

With regard to the copy of the Miracles, Duggan has argued persuasively that it was made from the exemplar originating in the priory of Christ Church in Canterbury sent by Abbot Odo of St Martin at Battle, Benedict's predecessor as prior of Christ Church, to two of his kinsmen at Igny in Flanders.[53] This exemplar never reached them owing to the 'deceit of the bearer,' which is about as much as we learn from a frustratingly vague letter sent by Odo to the same addressees, along with a replacement copy of the Miracles.[54] It is Odo's missing exemplar that ended up being copied in Lorvão in 1185, though by what mechanism it came to Portugal remains open to speculation.

The *Passio sancti Thome Cantuariensis archiepiscopi* which follows the Miracles is also of English origin but is otherwise unexceptional. Divided into lections and clearly intended for liturgical use, it appears to have been compiled by an unknown monastic author shortly after Becket's entry into the saintly pantheon.[55] The Becket letter, however, is not only remarkable but unique. It is a copy of a letter from Becket to Hyacinth, cardinal deacon of Stª Maria in Cosmedin, written in August 1169. Hyacinth had been one of Becket's most powerful supporters in his dispute with Henry II as is evinced by the correspondence between the two prelates.[56] It is not the contents of the letter, dealing with Becket's dispute with the Bishop of London, that concern us here but rather the circumstances of its arrival in Lorvão. In 1173, the same year of the translation of St Vincent's body to Lisbon, and in the very months of January

[52] Lisbon: Biblioteca Nacional de Portugal, MS Alc. CCXC/143.
[53] Anne J. Duggan, 'Aspects of Anglo-Portuguese Relations in the Twelfth Century: Manuscripts, Relics, Decretals and the Cult of St Thomas Becket at Lorvão, Alcobaça and Tomar', in A. J. Duggan (ed.), *Thomas Becket: Friends, Networks, Text and Cult* (Aldershot: Ashgate, 2007), Ch. X, pp. 1–19.
[54] Ibid., p. 5; J. C. Robertson and J. B. Sheppard (eds), *Materials for the History of Thomas Becket, Archbishop of Canterbury...*, Rolls Series 67, 7 vols (London: Longman, 1875–85), II (1876), xlix, n. A.
[55] Duggan, 'Aspects of Anglo-Portuguese Relations', p. 5.
[56] *The Correspondence of Thomas Becket, Archbishop of Canterbury 1162–1170*, ed. and trans. by Anne Duggan (Oxford: Oxford University Press, 2000), pp. 16, 118, 141, 217, 236, 305.

and February simultaneous with Becket's formal canonization, Hyacinth is attested in Coimbra and Braga as papal legate to Hispania. It is almost certain he visited, and probably stayed at, the royal monastery of S. Mamede de Lorvão, which is a mere six miles from Coimbra. Since the letter is not found in any of the many compilations of Becket's letters made in the twelfth century and since it is highly improbable that it had circulated with the Passion or the Miracles, we must suppose that the letter, now a prized relic of the new saint, was either given by Hyacinth to the monks of Lorvão, possibly as a token of gratitude for their hospitality, or that they deliberately solicited it from him, perhaps on behalf of their king and his stratagem of attraction.[57]

It was also during the 1170s that the cult of St Thomas was embraced by the Portuguese Templars. Master Gualdim Pais presided over the construction of the great Templar fortress at Tomar with its *rotunda* church, modelled on renowned buildings in Jerusalem, particularly the Church of the Holy Sepulchre. This *rotunda*, immediately dedicated to St Thomas, housed a small flask containing the brains of the martyr.[58] The association of the *rotunda*, physically indicative of the Holy City, with the Anglo-Norman St Thomas would have held strong resonances for crusaders from England.

Although there was a good deal of effort during the 1170s and 1180s to establish and promote the English cult of St Thomas in Portugal and whilst a small contingent of English participated in the conquest of Silves in 1189,[59] the Anglo-Normans do not feature again, after Lisbon in 1147, as major protagonists in the Portuguese conflict; certainly there is no record of them forming any significant body in the Alcácer campaign. Of course, during 1216 and 1217, whilst others were mobilizing for the Fifth Crusade, England was afflicted by dire civil war, the demands of which would have reduced the number of Anglo-Norman warriors available or inclined to undertake expeditionary operations. Yet there may have been another reason for their absence, namely that no further overtures were made to them following serious outbreaks of bad behaviour at Lisbon in the summer of 1190. In about early July of that year, a flotilla of 63 Anglo-Norman ships, part of Richard's fleet, arrived at Lisbon to take on supplies. While 500 good men went to help Sancho defend Santarém against the Almohads, many more of their shipmates went on the rampage in Lisbon, ill-treating and despoiling local Jewish and Muslim residents who had been granted special rights and privileges by Afonso Henriques after 1147. The ensuing riots only ended when Sancho's police arrested some 700 of the

---

[57] Duggan, 'Aspects of Anglo–Portuguese Relations', p. 6; Peter A. Newton, 'Some New Material for the Study of the Iconography of St Thomas Becket', in *Thomas Becket, Actes du colloque international de Sédières, 19–24 Août 1973*, ed. by Raymonde Foreville (Paris: Beauchesne, 1975), pp. 255–63; cf. R.A. Fletcher, 'Notes on the Early History of the Cult of St. Thomas Becket in Western Spain', in *Salamanca y Su Proyección en el Mundo*, ed. by José Antonio Bonilla Hernández (Salamanca: Gráficas Ortega, 1992), pp. 491–97 (p. 494): 'It may be that one of [Hyacinth's] many achievements was to introduce the churchmen of western Spain and Portugal to the church's new martyr.'

[58] Duggan, 'Aspects of Anglo–Portuguese Relations', p. 10.

[59] David, *Narratio de Itinere Navali*, p. 623.

mariners, forced them to make reparations and extracted undertakings from their leaders that discipline henceforth would be maintained, punishments enforced, and that rights and property would be respected whilst they were in the Portuguese kingdom, following which the fleet departed.[60] With the English crusaders having demonstrated a strong propensity for dangerous and unpredictable behaviour, the Portuguese seem to have thereafter regarded them with some suspicion and, perhaps not unreasonably, tactics of attraction were no longer enthusiastically applied in their direction.

---

[60] *The Annals of Roger de Hoveden*, trans. by Henry T. Riley, 2 vols (London: H. G. Bohn, 1853), II., pp. 148–50.

# An Inter-disciplinary Africanist: Patrick Chabal

DAVID BROOKSHAW

*University of Bristol*

Over the period of my career as a university teacher, which began in 1974 and ended in 2011, the profile of university departments changed substantially. As the product of an undergraduate course in the 1960s that combined literature and history in equal measure, I consider myself privileged to have been among a first generation of inter-disciplinary scholars. Yet my teachers belonged either to a department of language and literature or to a department of history. It was rare to find a historian in a language department, and Patrick was probably one of the first exceptions to the rule. It is ironical that a reorganization of the Portuguese Department at King's College London some years ago was to see him step sideways into a department that, on the surface, coincides more closely with what we had often assumed Patrick to be: a historian. Yet was he really a historian, at least in the traditional sense? The answer, as we are all aware, is clearly no. More than anything, perhaps, Patrick was an Africanist, who drew on diverse theories from the social sciences to buttress his own interpretations of African politics and political development. As he himself explains early on in his book, *Culture Troubles*, '[...] the most convincing comparative accounts of political processes are those that have combined solid historical research with the use of concepts from appropriate relevant other social sciences.'[1] [e.g. Anthropology — Clifford Geertz]. It is significant that Geertz was essentially a cultural anthropologist, and equally so that Patrick's most abiding intellectual trait was his attachment to the importance of culture in defining and explaining politics. Stemming, possibly, from his early study of Amílcar Cabral and the Guinean leader's Gramscian view of culture, it explains Patrick's equal interest in Lusophone African literatures, and his leading role in this field of study within British academia. Indeed, much of what Patrick developed in terms of his ideas about African literature in Portuguese harks back to his earlier work on Cabral, and his appreciation of this African leader's ideas: the importance of culture as being socially derived, the factors of cultural and ethnic diversity within borders arbitrarily drawn up by European colonial powers, and cultural adaptation. I shall illustrate this in due course when considering Patrick's contribution to the study of Lusophone African literature in British and, of

---

[1] Patrick Chabal and Jean-Pascal Daloz, *Culture Troubles* (London: Hurst, 2006), p. 27.

course, international academic circles. It is worth mentioning at this point that while individual African authors had been incorporated into the syllabuses of some university courses in Portuguese, in the early 1980s Patrick was the first specialist appointee in a Department where Portuguese was studied.

The 1970s and 80s — the period when Patrick would have been embarking on and completing his doctoral research and then teaching in the Department of Portuguese & Brazilian Studies at King's — were decades buffeted, with regard to Portuguese-speaking Africa, by our need to understand the two 'grand projects' affecting the five nations that eventually emerged from Portuguese colonialism. The first can loosely be defined as Lusotropicalism and its attendant notion of Portuguese exceptionality, the second, revolutionary Marxism as espoused by the leaders who took over from the Portuguese colonial governments in the Portuguese-speaking African countries as they became independent. Lusotropicalism would not, of course, suddenly die when Portuguese colonialism ended, any more than Marxist rhetoric (at least) stopped being uttered when countries like Angola and Mozambique began to turn their back on socialist revolutionary aspirations. Lusotropicalism lived on in the memories of those who had bought into Portuguese colonialism and now identified with its neocolonial echoes; Afro-Marxism lived on in the idealism of those who had bought into revolutionary socialism, many of whom had lived in Lusophone African countries during the 1970s and 80s as *co-operantes*, or aid workers. What Lusotropicalism and Marxism had in common was that they were overarching theories imposed on colonial and post-independence Lusophone Africa from outside, and in their different ways assumed that local culture either didn't exist at all, or was somehow backward and a hindrance to the desired modernity. Timeless notions of traditional African culture were thus circumscribed by equally timeless assumptions of Western superiority.

Generalizations about the cultures and literatures of Lusophone Africa tended therefore to be made in the early days. It was, of course, undeniable that there were certain common features to the literatures emerging from the five former Portuguese colonial territories in Africa, not least that they were all in Portuguese, and responded to similar outside literary influences and similar, albeit not identical, socio-economic features at home. But there were also profound differences between the cultural and social realities of these countries, not least between the offshore islands of São Tomé & Príncipe and Cape Verde and the continental countries of Guinea-Bissau, Angola and Mozambique, as well as among all of these. Patrick was able to satisfy the need for discrete study of the literatures of these countries, partly because the staffing of Portuguese and its curriculum at King's College allowed this, but partly out of intellectual conviction: comparative approaches to literature were fine, but they needed to be carried out on the basis of the deepest possible knowledge of the individual countries concerned. This, in turn, was the point of departure for the edited volume, *The Postcolonial Literature of Lusophone Africa*, which benefited from the expertise of five different contributors, including himself as leader of the project.

Linked to this, as well as to his other writings on politics and history, was his stated consciousness of the need to recognize the agency of the local, or indigenous, populations in the adaptation of their traditional culture to foreign influences. In this sense, Patrick posited a notion of a kind of hybridity that was the reverse of the Lusotropicalist ethos. The emphasis of the latter was on top-down assimilation: the notion that native populations could be raised into something called Portuguese civilization, and that cultural hybridity, in so far as it was acceptable (as in, for example, Freyre's Lusotropicalism), was heavily weighted towards the Portuguese side of the equation. But the absorption of foreign influences by traditional cultures, more akin, perhaps, to '*antropofagia*' as expounded by the Brazilian Modernists, placed indigenous populations in the driving seat of their own modernity, and even upset the time-honoured dichotomy between tradition and modernity (modernity as Westernization). Indeed, and again in *Culture Troubles*, Patrick suggests that modernization should be viewed as the process whereby traditional culture adapts to change, and he cites examples that are remarkably similar to the observations made by Mia Couto in his essays and texts of public intervention, vis-à-vis the traditional African culture of Mozambique: namely, the idea of an African witchdoctor using an old battery as a charm should be viewed as an expression of modernization. And Patrick had applied the same principles to his considerations about literature, when discussing so-called oral African culture and so-called modern written literature. In his introduction to *The Postcolonial Literature of Lusophone Africa*, he wrote: 'Africans, like everyone else, were able to decide for themselves how relevant European culture(s) were for their creative work. They could be inspired by good literature, whatever its origin, while still working to create their own "African" literature.'[2] To which he added: 'In reality, any culture is a constantly changing fusion of the traditional and the modern, so that modernity is not the reverse of tradition but rather tradition as it has changed and modernised. This is an important point, for much discussion on African literature has been vitiated by a focus on assumed and largely spurious contrasts between tradition and modernity.'[3]

The idea of the agency of practitioners of culture also explains his perception that literature should be studied not only in terms of the text, that is *textually*, but in terms of the social and political context in which it is written. Patrick, along with his countryman, Michel Laban, set store by the importance of writers' testimonies as being important to history, and more especially to the history of literature. His *Vozes Moçambicanas*, a collection of interviews with Mozambican writers of various generations, published in 1992, is a snapshot of cultural and literary life during a period of profound change in Mozambique,

---

[2] Patrick Chabal, *The Post-Colonial Literature of Lusophone Africa* (London: Hurst, 1996), p. 9.
[3] Ibid, p. 10.

the period broadly between 1985/86 and the peace accord of the early 1990s. However, unlike Laban's volumes on Cape Verde and Angola, in Patrick's book the interviewer's questions are removed, so what we have is a series of statements by Mozambican writers of the period, and the effect of this is that it is they who are being proactive in voicing their interpretations, rather than reactive by responding to questions (the interviewer is rendered invisible). But the principles outlined above — namely that outside influences are not imposed upon but absorbed and transformed by recipients — apply here. The reception of Brazilian Modernism, Portuguese Neo-Realism, Negritude, Black North American poetry and song, Afro-Cubanism, was inevitably filtered through Lisbon either in the form of books published there, books smuggled through there, or first read there by African students, but what is important is how these influences were understood by Mozambican and other Lusophone African writers, how they used these influences to chart their own literary evolution.

What Patrick seems to have captured is a process that could equally well apply to all those cultures that are caught on what is supposedly the wrong side of the fence that divides the so-called centre and the periphery, a concept that applied to the African colonies in relation to Portugal, but also applied to the self-elevated political powers of Northern Europe from the eighteenth century, in relation to the declining political and economic powers of the Iberian Peninsula. Just as African writers controlled what they absorbed from elsewhere, and re-packaged these influences into something original, so the same thing happened with writers of the *soi-disant* European periphery in relation to French, German and British literary influences. In this way, the multi-lingual, multi-cultural intellectuals of the so-called periphery, whether that periphery was Portugal or its colonies — the peripheries of a peripherical mother country — were, ironically, far more favourably equipped for modernity than the monoglots who were, and still are, so brazenly confident of their centrality. Perhaps the multi-lingual Frenchman, Patrick Chabal, could identify in a special way with these post-colonial, Portuguese-speaking African intellectuals.

# A Literature Waiting in the Wings for History: A Tribute to Patrick Chabal

MARGARIDA CALAFATE RIBEIRO

*Centro de Estudos Sociais, Universidade de Coimbra*

I would like to begin by making clear that I am an interloper on the terrain of Portuguese-language African literatures. Over my career, their varied manifestations have drawn me in, repeatedly revealing themselves to be key to my understanding of contemporary Portugal and its relationship with its former empire. I would like to register my profound gratitude to Patrick Chabal in particular, along with other colleagues and writers, who have shown me other means of expression, other archives and other ways of understanding those who centuries ago were startled by the unexpected arrival of a boat full of Europeans in the middle of the Indian Ocean. Indeed, Luís de Camões captured the curiosity in their bewilderment, as he had them question in their native tongues the Portuguese explorers:

> Comendo alegremente, perguntavam,
> Pela Arábica língua, donde vinham,
> Quem eram, de que terra, que buscavam,
> Ou que partes do mar corrido tinham?
>
> [As they ate contentedly, they began
> Questioning in the Arab language,
> — 'Where are you from? What do you
> Want? What oceans have you crossed?'][1]

Regardless of who discovered whom, an issue this passage undoubtedly raises, I am more interested in highlighting the fact that the questions the natives posed, in an apparently naive way, are central to the identity of the people Portugal's adventurers came across. From the moment of first contact, one of the longest and most asymmetrical dialogues in memory was begun.

That asymmetry has always troubled me. Where are the texts from this long, tense and essentially deaf dialogue? Where are the texts that interrogate the European condition? Where are the texts that describe territories beyond a European gaze? Where are the texts written in languages beyond Portuguese?

In the margins of an apparently hegemonic Eurocentric discourse, there

---

[1] Luís de Camões, *Os Lusíadas* (Lisbon: Instituto Camões, 1992), from Canto I, Stanza 50 (p. 13); Luis Vaz de Camões, *The Lusíads*, translation, introduction and notes by Landeg White (Oxford and New York: Oxford University Press, 1997), p. 13.

were always signs that bore witness to the existence of other ethno-cultural subjects. The conditions of their enunciation were plunged into silence during colonialism, as Spivak points out in her seminal article 'Can the subaltern speak?' (1988). Today, historians, literary critics and scholars must rescue those other discourses from the margins of colonial rhetoric where other histories do exist. These histories underpin the first texts in Portuguese in the literatures of São Tomé, Guinea-Bissau, Angola, Mozambique and Cape Verde. They are texts that inscribe a cultural difference that would eventually mature into a demand for independence. That is why literary scholars, in particular of Portuguese-language African culture, reflect in their studies on the intrinsic relationship between politics and literature. Field-founders like Manuel Ferreira, Alfredo Margarido, Maria Aparecida Santilli, Michel Laban, Russell Hamilton, Gerald Moser, Irene Guerra Marques, Laura Padilha, Benjamim Abdala Júnior, and José Luandino Vieira, as well as the generation that followed them, including Pires Laranjeira, Rita Chaves, Fátima Mendonça, Tânia Macedo, Moema Parente Augel, David Brookshaw, Patrick Chabal, Inocência Mata, Ana Mafalda Leite, Francisco Noa, Gilberto Matusse, Odete Costa Semedo, Phillip Rothwell, Hilary Owen among so many others, understood the key role of literature in an understanding of history, from the moment the Portuguese arrived in Africa, throughout their long colonial presence, and the struggles for independence. Even today, the relationship remains strong.

Among the many people who taught me to look at those literatures, Patrick Chabal occupies pride of place. I had the privilege of working with him as a doctoral student and then as a colleague. Like me, Patrick was not a specialist in the literatures of Portuguese-language Africa. He wasn't even a literary scholar. Rather, he was a historian and political scientist who quickly understood the importance of these literatures for his work. He understood them as profoundly linked to political processes. He saw them as a literature inherently linked to history, in fact, a literature waiting in the wings for history, as we can see in the themes he developed in his introduction to *The Postcolonial Literature of Lusophone Africa*. We need only remember José Luandino Vieira's literary project to understand how the language of colonization and oppression (as indeed Portuguese was) can be transformed into the language of liberation. We need only remember the Angolan, Pepetela's literary project to understand literature as the recreation of a historiographical imagination, from its precolonial foundational myths in *Lueji*, through the Dutch occupation resisted by Angolans and Portuguese in *A Gloriosa Família*, and the modern colonial era and its end in *Yaka*, right up to the present day in *Predadores*. Likewise, we just have to remember a book like Manuel Rui's *A Casa do Rio* or João Paulo Borges Coelho's *A Crónica da Rua 513.5* to feel completely decolonization's fracturing of the historical process and of the subjectivities of those who played a leading role in it. Here is where history and literature join forces, not just as mutual sources, but through the possibilities literature offers for representing those moments in individual histories that fuse with the collective history of a people. Those moments produce subjectivities, feelings, emotions — none of which history can capture, or give. That was the essential aspect Patrick Chabal understood from his own discipline, looking out on literatures that were so viscerally connected to politics and history. That is why in 1996, when he launched *The Postcolonial Literature of Lusophone Africa*, he wrote in his introduction about the importance of language and metropolitan culture in the development of these literatures. He rejected simplistic and dated views, formed on the coat-tails of a legitimate political rejection of colonialism. He understood that rejection should not include a complete denial of the former metropolis's culture as a decisive influence that actually enabled the development of postcolonial literatures. For Patrick Chabal, the denial of a dual legacy — both Western and African — is both analytically sterile and politically weak. The importance of Patrick Chabal's pioneering work is its link to fundamental issues about the elaboration of the histories of literature, handbooks or readers, and consequently to the canons these form. Understanding the inclusion and exclusion of writers, at the heart of the conception of histories of literature, anthologies and collections of texts, was crucial to him. Patrick Chabal shows the permeability of literature as a genre, and its power to include as foundational texts, historiographical sources, which are themselves unique moments in literature. We just need to remember the inception of Brazilian literature with the Letter by Pêro Vaz de Caminha as proof. He also raised the question of cultural and literary temporality linked to the political and cultural identity of a country. Finally, he raised the question of determining from which space literature speaks — what the place of its enunciation is. In essence, the question Patrick Chabal pioneers is the paradox of literary nationalisms, characterized by including and excluding authors, mixing political and economic reasons with historical, literary and aesthetic ones. As these nationalisms do this, they risk eliminating something that constitutes their very identity: the long colonial presence. In this, Patrick Chabal echoes other scholars and writers, who point to what José Luandino Vieira would come to call the 'black holes' of Angolan literature, things as simple as deciding where to place colonial literature, and writers working prior to what became Angola. Deciding where to place writers in the diaspora. To ask ourselves what, at the end of the day, Angolan or Mozambican literature *is*, how to teach it, and how to interpret it.

That is why the post-independence generation of literary critics has concentrated not just on narrating the histories of these literatures, following the traditional European model of periodization, but rather on identifying the literary object of these new nations and thus contributing to the construction of a possible canon by identifying what Antonio Candido, in reference to Brazilian literature, termed a 'literary system'. Patrick Chabal's cornerstone contribution in *The Postcolonial Literature of Lusophone Africa*, beyond spreading its study in the English-speaking world and thus enabling more comparative studies of the African continent, is his sensitivity to literature as a space to understand subjectivities inherent to historical processes. Liberation thus becomes entwined with the nation's language and with the need to create an alternative narrative to that of the colonizer.

As he asserts, in the modern era, the most visible expression of narratives opposed to the colonizer's was the grand narrative engendered by the anticolonial struggle. It focused on a denunciation of colonialism and its vices and on the elaboration of a future national project. Through this narrative, more focused on hope for the future than a revision of the past, more Eurocentric than nationalist and indigenous, the idea of Angola for the Angolans and Mozambique for the Mozambicans was born. This would come to be known as Angolanness, Mozambicanness, Cape Verdeanness, etc. As Patrick Chabal points out, the appeal to post-independence equality, taken to extremes by the single party, caused the dramatic erasure of differences that formed the social and cultural fabric of the recently freed countries. It was contradictory. Often, it was synonymous with a continuation of the imperial mechanisms whose influence continued to be felt, even if it was not initially so obvious in the euphoria of the revolutionary moment, whipped up by literature. In fact, combat literature was an armed wing, encouraging the struggle for the nation-to-be by inventing a single past, from which Guineans, Mozambicans and Angolans could emerge and move forward united without any cracks or differences, against a common enemy: colonization and its legacies. Portuguese was the language of symbolic representation for what were conceived as nation-states as drafted by their first leaders. This decision guaranteed a cultural identity particularly in Angola and Mozambique in their southern African context, by reducing their linguistic complexity to a State expressed only in Portuguese. At the same time, it relegated to the background the languages of many different peoples. Patrick Chabal, over his career, raised the questions: how do we situate the idea of the nation, brought into being through an anticolonial struggle, in relation to other grand narratives such as race, religion, ethnicity and gender? What is their place vis-à-vis the 'new' discursive hegemony of the national project?

These questions, raised by a historian of Africa whose language was not Portuguese, were fundamental for our critical gaze on these literatures, and once again it was to literature that Patrick Chabal went in search for answers. It was through literary expression in Portuguese, in theatre, sculpture and painting, that other perspectives emerged. At the same time as it nurtured and strengthened the national project, it also opened up alternatives to the political hegemony. In sum, literature began rejecting, amending or questioning the hegemony of the national project, interrogating its value as representative of a nation that simultaneously ruptures from the state. That is why some writers and artists tried in their work to make sense of the violence and destruction inflicted on their countries, assailed by the immensity of multiple wars. That is the only way to understand the hatred and repulsion expressed in José Craveirinha's *Babalaze das Hienas*, or Rui Knopfli's tragic poetic feeling, or José Luandino Vieira's literary silence, or Odete Semedo's unanswered questions. Quietly, a younger generation developed their own literary projects, including Mia Couto, Ungulani Ba Ka Khosa, Luís Carlos Patraquim, Lilia Momplé, Eduardo White, João Paulo Borges Coelho, Paulina Chiziane, Ana Paula Tavares, João de Melo, João Maimona, José Luis Mendonça, Abdulai Sila, Tony Tcheka, Conceição Lima among many others. They challenged from different perspectives and in various hues the macro-narrative of a single voice. They offered multiple voices that belied the fallacy of rigid, geographical and cultural boundaries with which many insisted on wrapping up the literary imagination of the nation. Patrick Chabal, with Ana Mafalda Leite, David Brookshaw, Moema Parente Augel and Caroline Shaw, brought these texts to the English-speaking world, in a work that today is a key reference worldwide because of the many questions it raises. It is a heritage of reflection for all scholars of Portuguese-language African literatures, literatures duly individuated in the volume.

In this vein of deploying a multidisciplinary and political approach in the analysis of Portuguese-language African literatures, I organized at Coimbra's Social Studies Centre, where I work, courses on each of these nations' literatures. These led to several books to which professors of literature, historians, political scientists, colleagues from law, anthropology and sociology contributed: *Lendo Angola* (2008), *Moçambique: das palavras escritas* (2008), *Literaturas da Guiné-Bissau: cantando os escritos da história* (2011), *Literaturas Insulares: leituras e escritas de Cabo Verde e S. Tomé e Príncipe* (2011). Together, both speakers and non-speakers of Portuguese entered into dialogue with themes and terrain that Patrick Chabal's work had first ploughed.

*Translated by Phillip Rothwell*

# Abstracts

*Eros, Love and the (Anti-) Lyric in João Cabral*
MARTA PEIXOTO
ABSTRACT. To his last days, João Cabral claimed as a badge of honour his status as an anti-lyric poet, assessing correctly the momentous contribution of this aspect of his poetry to Brazilian and world literature. The critical bibliography on Cabral has followed suit, paying particular attention to Cabral's anti-lyricism, but it should also be noted that a significant portion of Cabral's poetry does not, in fact, turn its back on the lyric. Instead, it is in dialogue with — and perhaps confronts — certain significant aspects of the lyric, achieving 'um lirismo de tensões' [a lyricism of tensions] (João Alexandre Barbosa). This paper explores the particular lyricism of Cabral's poetry about eros and love by sketching a chronological development from *Pedra do sono* (1942) to *Sevilha andando* (1992) and by examining in some detail the strategies of a few representative poems. It argues that an important portion of Cabral's poetry, including a number of his most luminous poems, can best be understood in the context of the lyrical tradition, to which they make a strikingly original contribution.
KEYWORDS. João Cabral, lyric, images of women.

RESUMO. Até seus últimos dias, João Cabral defendeu seu estatuto de anti-lírico, avaliando corretamente a grande contribuição que este aspecto de sua poesia deu à literatura brasileira e mundial. A bibliografia crítica sobre Cabral também tem dado atenção ao caráter anti-lírico de sua poética. No entanto, é importante notar que grande parte da poesia cabralina não ignora a lírica, mas dialoga e quiçá entra em confronto com certo aspectos significativos da lírica, chegando a 'um lirismo de tensões' (segundo João Alexandre Barbosa). Assim, este artigo analisa o lirismo peculiar de Cabral ligado a eros e ao amor, mapeando o desenvolvimento do tema desde *Pedra do sono* (1942) até *Sevilha andando* (1992), examinando detalhadamente as estratégias poéticas de algumas das poesias mais representativas. O artigo defende que uma parcela importante da poesia cabralina, inclusive algumas de suas composições mais significativas, podem ser entendidas melhor no contexto da tradição lírica, à qual trazem uma contribuição marcante.
PALAVRAS-CHAVE. João Cabral, poesia lírica, imagens de mulheres.

## Journeys and Landscapes in João Cabral de Melo Neto
SARA BRANDELLERO

ABSTRACT. This article focuses on the theme of the journey and renditions of landscape in two of João Cabral's key works from the 1950s, *O cão sem plumas* (1950) and *O rio* (1954). The writing of these works coincided with the beginning of Cabral's critical engagement with the grave social reality of his native North-East Brazil. Thus, it will analyse the significance of Cabral's treatment of landscape and of the interconnectivity it seeks out between the human and nonhuman worlds, as his poetry searches for ethical solutions.

KEYWORDS. João Cabral, *O cão sem plumas*, *O rio*, *Morte e vida severina*, literature and landscape, nonhuman.

RESUMO. Este artigo se detém sobre o tema da viagem e o tratamento da paisagem na poesia de João Cabral, dedicando atenção especial a dois poemas chave da década de 1950: *O cão sem plumas* (1950) e *O rio* (1954). Estas duas obras coincidiram com o início de uma trajetória de poesia engajada por parte do Cabral, desde então fortemente comprometido com a crítica à grave realidade social do Nordeste brasileiro. Desta forma, o artigo se debruça sobre o lugar da paisagem na poesia cabralina e as conexões que ela estabelece entre o humano e o não-humano, em sua busca por soluções éticas.

PALAVRAS-CHAVE. João Cabral, *O cão sem plumas*, *O rio*, *Morte e vida severina*, literatura e paisagem, não-humano.

## Epistolary Connections: João Cabral and Murilo Mendes
CARLOS MENDES DE SOUSA

ABSTRACT. This essay provides a study of a collection of unpublished letters between João Cabral de Melo Neto and fellow Modernist poet, and literary master, Murilo Mendes (1901–1975). The epistolary exchange helps to map the biographical and literary journeys of these two authors. The friendship and literary dialogues between these two distinctive voices provide insight into their points of contact — one example of which is their unconditional passion for Spain and Spanish culture. Cabral's reflections on flamenco, for instance, help us increase our understanding of his poetics, and we find a significant group of letters covering the origins of his collection *Quaderna*, a book which he dedicated to Murilo Mendes.

KEYWORDS. João Cabral, Murilo Mendes, Spain, Flamenco, *Quaderna*.

RESUMO. O presente ensaio incide na leitura de um conjunto de cartas inéditas entre João Cabral de Melo Neto e Murilo Mendes (1901–1975). Alguns dados apresentados nesta epistolografia ajudam-nos a perspetivar os percursos biográficos e literários dos dois autores (os lugares e as referências de eleição). A amizade e as conversas literárias entre dois poetas tão diferentes têm vários pontos de contacto. Refira-se em particular a paixão incondicional pela Espanha e pelas coisas espanholas; destaque-se a este respeito as reflexões de Cabral sobre o flamenco que nos ajudam a compreender a sua poética. Encontramos ainda um significativo conjunto de cartas à volta da génese de *Quaderna*, livro que foi dedicado a Murilo.

PALAVRAS-CHAVE. João Cabral, Murilo Mendes, Spain, Flamenco, Quaderna.

## 'Auto do frade' by João Cabral de Melo Neto: A Trope of the Passion
VINICIUS MARIANO DE CARVALHO

ABSTRACT. This article provides an analysis of the one-act play, *Auto do frade*, by João Cabral de Melo Neto, as a trope of the Passion of Christ, focusing particularly on the speeches of Frei Caneca in the poem. The analysis compares these speeches with the seven words of Christ on the cross, providing a new perspective on the play. The article demonstrates how the poet captures remarkable elements of the Carmelite mystical tradition and translates them into this dramatic poem. Finally, the article relates this poem to Cabral's earlier play *Morte e vida severina*, in which a dialogue with religious motifs is also evident.

KEYWORDS. *Auto do frade*, poetry and religion, Frei Caneca, João Cabral de Melo Neto.

RESUMO. Este artigo faz uma análise hermenêutica do *Auto do frade*, de João Cabral de Melo Neto, como um tropo da Paixão de Cristo, especialmente com foco nas falas de Frei Caneca no poema. A análise compara estas falas às sete palavras de Cristo na cruz e dentro desta perspetiva traça qual o horizonte exegético que se pode depreender no poema. O artigo mostra como o poeta capta elementos fortes da tradição mística carmelita e os traduz neste poema dramático, bem como relaciona este poema a *Morte e vida severina*, em que também se evidencia um diálogo com motivos de caráter religioso.

PALAVRAS-CHAVE. *Auto do frade*, poesia e religião, Frei Caneca, João Cabral de Melo Neto.

## The Extreme and Geometry: Notes on João Cabral de Melo Neto's Collection on Bullfighting and his Poetic Imagery
FLORA SÜSSEKIND

ABSTRACT. This essay takes as its starting point a small collection of newspaper cuttings, photographs and periodicals from the 1940s and 50s, which belonged to João Cabral de Melo Neto and remained in his apartment on the Praia do Flamengo for decades. At the time when his heirs disposed of part of his library and of some old papers and periodicals, this material ended up in the Berinjela Bookshop in Rio de Janeiro where, perhaps due to its poor state of preservation, it did not find any immediate purchasers and, given my interest, was eventually offered to me by the booksellers as a gift. What we have, in fact, is a mini-collection of photographic records and essayistic commentaries about certain bullfighters and bullfights, articles about theories of bullfighting, about breeds of cattle, tragic bullfighters, fairs, and peculiar forms of bullfighting. The examination of these items allows us to contextualize certain images from Cabral's work (geometry, grim resignation, the play between tangency and deviation) in the poems about Spain, bullfights and certain bullfighters. And it points directly towards his particular preference for Manolete, but also for Murilo González, Lagartija and Gallito, among other bullfighters. These figures, images and tauromachy, which were all intensely present in the cultural panorama of the mid-twentieth century (see Leiris, Hemingway, Picasso etc.), were nevertheless to fulfil a particular function in Cabral's poetics.

KEYWORDS. João Cabral de Melo Neto, tauromachy, bullfighters, Spain, Manolete.

RESUMO. Este ensaio tem como ponto de partida um pequeno conjunto de recortes de jornal, de fotos e de periódicos dos anos 1940 e 1950, que pertenceu a João Cabral de Melo Neto e permaneceu guardado em seu apartamento da Praia do Flamengo por décadas. Na época em que seus herdeiros se desfizeram de parte da sua biblioteca e de alguns papéis velhos e periódicos, esse material foi parar na Livraria Beringela, no Rio de Janeiro, onde, talvez devido ao seu mau estado de conservação, não encontrou compradores imediatos, e, diante do meu interesse, acabou sendo oferecido a mim, como um presente, pelos livreiros. Trata-se, na verdade, de uma mini-coleção de registros fotográficos e crônicas sobre determinados toureiros e touradas, artigos sobre teorias do toureio, sobre ganaderías, toureiros trágicos, feiras, e formas peculiares de tourear. A observação desses guardados permite a contextualização de certas imagens cabralinas (a geometria, a severa resignação, o jogo entre tangência e desvio) nos poemas sobre a Espanha, as touradas e certos toureiros. E aponta diretamente para sua preferência, em especial, por Manolete, mas também por Murilo González, Lagartija, Gallito, dentre outros toureiros. Personagens, imagens e tauromaquia que estavam intensamente presentes no panorama cultural de meados do século XX (vide Leiris, Hemingway, Picasso, etc.) cumpririam, no entanto, função particular na poética cabralina.

PALAVRAS-CHAVE. João Cabral de Melo Neto, tauromaquia, toureiros, Espanha, Manolete.

*Tactics of Attraction: Saints, Pilgrims and Warriors in the Portuguese Reconquista*

JONATHAN WILSON

ABSTRACT. This paper considers aspects of the Portuguese Reconquista highlighting the collaboration of maritime crusaders en route to Palestine in the conquests of Lisbon, Silves and Alcácer do Sal. It proposes that elements more or less connected to the Portuguese royal courts of Afonso Henriques, Sancho I and Afonso II developed and prosecuted a policy for attracting crusaders passing along the Atlantic coast to join military operations on the Portuguese-Andalusi frontier. The policy operated through the promotion of various saintly cults, the representation of Portugal as part of the pilgrimage route to Jerusalem, and the advancement of the notion that the Portuguese war on the Andalusi Saracens offered opportunities for Christian martyrdom on a par with the Crusades in the East. The pinnacle of this strategy was achieved during preparations for the conquest of Alcácer do Sal, in 1217.

KEYWORDS. Crusades, pilgrimage, Reconquest, St Vincent, Lisbon, Silves, Alcácer-do-Sal, Soeiro-Viegas, St Thomas Becket.

RESUMO. Este artigo aborda aspectos da reconquista portuguesa, destacando a colaboração de cruzados marítimos a caminho da Palestina nas conquistas de Lisboa, Silves e Alcácer do Sal. Propõe que elementos mais ou menos vinculados às cortes reais portuguesas de Afonso Henriques, Sancho I e Afonso II elaboraram e implementaram uma política de atraírem os cruzados que passavam pelo litoral atlântico a participarem das operações militares na fronteira portuguesa-andaluza. A política se efetuou promovendo diversos cultos santos, representando Portugal como parte da rota de peregrinação rumo a Jerusalém, e afirmando a noção de que a guerra dos portugueses contra os sarracenos andaluzes apresentaria oportunidades para o martírio cristão que se igualavam às Cruzadas no Oriente. Alcançou-se o cúmulo dessa estratégia durante as preparações para a conquista de Alcácer do Sal em 1217.

PALAVRAS-CHAVE. Cruzadas, peregrinação, Reconquista, São Vicente, Lisboa, Silves, Alcácer-do-Sal, Soeiro-Viegas, São Tomás Becket.

*An Inter-disciplinary Africanist: Patrick Chabal*

DAVID BROOKSHAW

ABSTRACT. This essay assesses the originality of Patrick Chabal's contribution to the interdisciplinary study of Lusophone Africa in two major senses: as a political scientist, historian and pioneer of Lusophone African literary studies who understood not only how the continent's distinctive political culture should inform the reading of its literatures, but also that culture in its turn must be central to explaining the politics of the region; and above all as an Africanist, who grasped the need to appreciate the agency of Africans in their self-transformation amidst the forces of tradition and modernity and the dual ideological legacies of Lusotropicalism and Afro-Marxism.

KEYWORDS. Patrick Chabal, Lusophone Africa, culture, tradition, modernity, Lusotropicalism, Marxism.

RESUMO. Este ensaio avalia a originalidade da contribuição de Patrick Chabal ao estudo interdisciplinar da África lusófona em dois sentidos principais: enquanto estudioso da ciência política, historiador e pioneiro dos estudos literários da África lusófona, que entendeu não apenas como a cultura política distinta do continente deveria informar a leitura das suas literaturas, mas também que a cultura por sua vez deveria ser decisiva para explicar a política da região; e sobretudo enquanto africanista, que percebeu a necessidade de compreender a agência dos africanos na sua auto-transformação em meio às forças da tradição e da modernidade e à herança ideológica dupla do lusotropicalismo e do afro-marxismo.

PALAVRAS-CHAVE. Patrick Chabal, África lusófona, cultura, tradição, modernidade, lusotropicalismo, marxismo.

## A Literature Waiting in the Wings for History: A Tribute to Patrick Chabal
MARGARIDA CALAFATE RIBEIRO

ABSTRACT. This essay focuses on Patrick Chabal's specific perspective towards the study of Lusophone African literature and its crucial role in shaping the broader field of the discipline, by drawing attention to the historical importance of the subaltern, indigenous voice as a protagonist in the struggle for liberation. His legacy, not only to students of literature and culture, but also to historians, political scientists, lawyers, anthropologist and sociologists, is to demonstrate how the multiple voices of literary expression have challenged the univocal macro-narratives of postcolonial history. Whether in the contradictions of canon formation, the struggles over national languages and narratives, or the critiques of the political project, the nations' ruptures with the state, and their experience of violence in war, Patrick Chabal's work has illuminated the dialogue between literature and history in the complex unfolding of the postcolonial experience.

KEYWORDS. Patrick Chabal, Lusophone Africa, nationalism, subaltern, narrative, postcolonial, language.

RESUMO. Este ensaio debruça-se sobre a perspectiva específica de Patrick Chabal em relação ao estudo da literatura da África lusófona e o papel decisivo dela ao formar o campo mais amplo da disciplina, chamando a atenção para a importância histórica da voz subalterna, indígena como protagonista da luta pela libertação. Seu legado, não apenas para os estudiosos da literatura e da cultura, mas também para os historiadores, os especialistas da ciência política, do direito, da antropologia e da sociologia, é o de demonstrar como as vozes múltiplas da expressão literária têm contestado as macro-narrativas univocais da história pós-colonial. Seja nas contradições da formação dos cânones, seja nas lutas pelas línguas e narrativas nacionais, seja nas críticas do projeto político, nas rupturas da nação com o estado e na experiência da violência na guerra, a contribuição de Patrick Chabal é a de iluminar o diálogo entre a literatura e a história no desdobrar-se complexo da experiência pós-colonial.

PALAVRAS-CHAVE. Patrick Chabal, África lusófona, nacionalismo, subalterno, narrativa, póscolonial, língua.

www.ingramcontent.com/pod-product-compliance
Lightning Source LLC
Chambersburg PA
CBHW050601300426
44112CB00013B/2012